CULTURES OF THE WORLD

Haiti

Cavendish
Square

New York

Published in 2016 by Cavendish Square Publishing, LLC
243 5th Avenue, Suite 136, New York, NY 10016
Copyright © 2016 by Cavendish Square Publishing, LLC

Third Edition

Library of Congress Cataloging-in-Publication Data

NgCheong-Lum, Roseline, 1962- author.
Haiti / Roseline NgCheong-Lum, Leslie Jermyn and Debbie Nevins.
pages cm. — (Cultures of the world)
Includes bibliographical references and index.
ISBN 978-1-5026-0802-4 (hardcover) ISBN 978-1-5026-0803-1 (ebook)
1. Haiti—Juvenile literature. I. Jermyn, Leslie, author. II. Nevins, Debbie, author. III. Title.

F1915.2.N43 2016
972.94—dc23

2015035323

Writers, Roseline Ng Cheong-Lum, Leslie Jermyn; Debbie Nevins, third edition
Editorial Director, third edition: David McNamara
Editor, third edition: Debbie Nevins
Art Director, third edition: Jeffrey Talbot
Designer, third edition: Jessica Nevins
Production Manager, third edition Jennifer Ryder-Talbot
Cover Picture Researcher: Stephanie Flecha
Picture Researcher, third edition: Jessica Nevins

PICTURE CREDITS

The photographs in this book are used with the permission of: Leanne Walker/Lonely Planet Images/Getty Images, cover; arindambanerjee/Shutterstock.com, 1; Hank Shiffman/Shutterstock.com, 3; arindambanerjee/Shutterstock.com, 5; Jan Sochor/Latincontent/Getty Images, 6; arindambanerjee/Shutterstock.com, 7; arindambanerjee/Shutterstock.com, 8; Daniel-Alvarez/Shutterstock.com, 9; Tuangtong Soraprasert/Shutterstock.com, 10; Peter Hermes Furian/Shutterstock.com, 11; BigDaveBo/Shutterstock.com, 12; James P. Blair/National Geographic/Getty Images, 13; KSK Imaging/Shutterstock.com, 14; VANDERLEI ALMEIDA/AFP/Getty Images, 16; John Scofield/National Geographic/Getty Images, 18; cph 3b07443/loc.gov, 20; Culture Club/Getty Images, 21; Auguste Raffet/Histoire de Napoleon, M. de Norvins, 1839, page 239/File:Haitian Revolution.jpg/Wikimedia Commons, 23; Martinet (del.)-Masson (Sculp.)/FRANCE MILITAIRE/File:Incendie de la Plaine du Cap.-Massacre des Blancs par les Noirs. FRANCE MILITAIRE.-Martinet del.-Masson Sculp-33.jpg/Wikimedia Commons, 24; NYPL Digital Gallery/File:Général Toussaint Louverture.jpg/Wikimedia Commons, 26; Hulton Archive/Getty Images, 28; The Times/Gallo Images/Getty Images, 29; AFP/AFP/Getty Images, 30; Harvey Meston/Getty Images, 32; HECTOR RETAMAL/AFP/Getty Images, 34; arindambanerjee/Shutterstock.com, 35; Paul Stringer/Shutterstock.com, 36; HECTOR RETAMAL/AFP/Getty Images, 38; Everett Historical/Shutterstock.com, 40; Nuk2013/Shutterstock.com, 41; HECTOR RETAMAL/AFP/Getty Images, 42; glenda/Shutterstock.com, 43; Logan Abassi/MINUSTAH via Getty Images, 44; THONY BELIZAIRE/AFP/Getty Images, 46; HECTOR RETAMAL/AFP/Getty Images, 48; Mass Communication Specialist 2nd Class JBryan Weyers/U.S. Navy via Getty Images, 49; HECTOR RETAMAL/AFP/Getty Images, 50; HECTOR RETAMAL/AFP/Getty Images, 51; HECTOR RETAMAL/AFP/Getty Images, 52; THONY BELIZAIRE/AFP/Getty Images, 53; STAN HONDA/AFP/Getty Images, 54; HECTOR RETAMAL/AFP/Getty Images, 55; Rafael Sanchez Fabres/LatinContent/Getty Images, 56; Nolte Lourens/Shutterstock.com, 57; THONY BELIZAIRE/AFP/Getty Images, 58; Universal History Archive/UIG via Getty Images, 60; Maciej Czekajewski/Shutterstock.com, 61; Stephen Chernin/Getty Images, 62; arindambanerjee/Shutterstock.com,63; ROBERTO SCHMIDT/AFP/Getty Images, 64; Universal Images Group via Getty Images, 66; iew Pictures/UIG via Getty Images, 67; HECTOR RETAMAL/AFP/Getty Images, 69; VANDERLEI ALMEIDA/AFP/Getty Images, 70; arindambanerjee/Shutterstock.com, 71; Michelle D. Milliman/Shutterstock.com, 72; Marco Di Lauro/Edit by Getty Images, 73; Joe Raedle/Getty Images, 76; HECTOR RETAMAL/AFP/Getty Images, 77; Joe Raedle/Getty Images, 78; Joe Raedle/Getty Images, 79; HECTOR RETAMAL/AFP/Getty Images, 80; Dario Mitidieri/Getty Images, 81; THONY BELIZAIRE/AFP/Getty Images, 82; Markus Matzel/ullstein bild via Getty Images, 83; HECTOR RETAMAL/AFP/Getty Images, 86; Carolyn Cole/Los Angeles Times via Getty Images, 87; AP Phtoo/Michael Stravato, 89; Daniel-Alvarez/Shutterstock.com, 90; AP Photo/Ramon Espinosa, 91; Spencer Platt/Getty Images, 93; Jerritt Clark/WireImage, 94; HECTOR RETAMAL/AFP/Getty Images, 95; Jan Sochor/Latincontent/Getty Images, 96; HECTOR RETAMAL/AFP/Getty Images, 97; HECTOR RETAMAL/AFP/Getty Images, 98; Ernesto Ruscio/Getty Images, 100; HECTOR RETAMAL/AFP/Getty Images, 101; HECTOR RETAMAL/AFP/Getty Images, 102; CLAUDIO SANTANA/AFP/Getty Images, 103; John Seaton Callahan/Moment/Getty Images, 104; HECTOR RETAMAL/AFP/Getty Images, 106; arindambanerjee/Shutterstock.com, 108; HECTOR RETAMAL/AFP/Getty Images, 110; THONY BELIZAIRE/AFP/Getty Images, 112; THONY BELIZAIRE/AFP/Getty Images, 113; THONY BELIZAIRE/AFP/Getty Images, 114; THONY BELIZAIRE/AFP/Getty Images, 115; THONY BELIZAIRE/AFP/Getty Images, 116; HECTOR RETAMAL/AFP PHOTO/Getty Images, 117; THONY BELIZAIRE/AFP/Getty Images, 121; THONY BELIZAIRE/AFP/Getty Images, 122; THONY BELIZAIRE/AFP/Getty Images, 123; THONY BELIZAIRE/AFP/Getty Images, 124; Melanie Stetson Freeman/The Christian Science Monitor via Getty Images, 125; jazz3311/Shutterstock.com, 126; Fabricio UZ/Shutterstock.com, 127; View Pictures/UIG via Getty Images, 128; View Pictures/UIG via Getty Images, 129; Charlotte Lake/Shutterstock.com, 130; Aleksandra Duda/Shutterstock.com, 131.

PRECEDING PAGE

A young girl laughs outside her tent a few months after the earthquake.

Printed in the United States of America

CONTENTS

HAITI TODAY

TO BE A HAITIAN TODAY IS TO KNOW DIFFICULTY. IN A LAND full of natural beauty, that beauty is often overshadowed by the hardships of those living within it. Haiti is the poorest country in the Western Hemisphere. Despite its troubles, however, it is a country beloved by its people, even while most of them struggle to meet the basic necessary means for their lives.

As the first free republic to have a majority population of people of color, there was great hope for the post-colonial era. Unfortunately, that anticipation has been dulled by centuries of mismanagement of natural resources, political corruption, and institutionalized racism against the vast majority black population.

Haitian society has a strongly enforced class system with whites and mulattoes (people of mixed white and black races) holding the vast majority of wealth and power within society. Those descended from Africans make up 95 percent of the population. They live almost exclusively in poverty. There is very little crossover between the two groups and therefore very little incentive for those in power to share with the less fortunate, especially as black citizens have been historically considered inferior. This unwillingness to work with and help the poor has only served to strengthen the divide and drive the country more deeply into debt and general destitution.

Despite these privations, Haiti has built itself a unique culture by deftly combining the sometimes-opposing forces that shaped its creation. While Roman Catholicism was the official state religion until 2003, the African polytheism of vodou flourished in an unofficial capacity, until it was recognized as a second, equal official faith. It is said that in Haiti, almost everyone practices Catholicism, but *everyone* practices vodou. Catholicism looms large over the cultural landscape and its influence is brought to bear on the wealthy minority, but the majority poor hews more faithfully to the vodou practices, though they celebrate the Christian holidays with full-throated enthusiasm.

Despite the adversity, Haitians are known as a group of people that make do with what they have, celebrate what they can, and improve their lot where possible. In many cases this involves a commitment to art, as evidenced by taptaps. These are old Japanese-made trucks or vans that have been

A taptap bus passes through downtown Port-au-Prince.

converted into public buses. Painted with images of mermaids, animals, flowers, or futuristic spaceships, they look more like circus wagons. Decorations on a truck body may include stars, diamonds, and squiggles in red, green, and gold. The more flamboyant the artwork, the higher the driver's status.

There are hundreds of painters in Haiti, many working with gaudy color palettes. Most are self-taught, working to bring some measure of levity and cheer to their work. Often, the work is in the Primitive style, a deliberately imperfect method that presents portraits of everyday Haitians, capturing the truth of their lives as filtered through the artists' eyes and brushes. Murals are also a popular style, adorning everything from cathedrals to bus stations.

An artist paints outside of his tent in Port-au-Prince in August 2010. In the background, young men are playing chess.

Even Haiti's cuisine is informed by its place at the societal crossroads. With its reliance on local produce, its Latin-Caribbean roots favor well-spiced, boldly flavored dishes that nod to the traditions brought from Africa. However, the delicate sophistication present in traditional French cooking has worked its way into local dishes in the form of, for example, subtle sauces.

Haitians do find time to celebrate, and their holidays are affairs of great import. From the ritual of Midnight Mass and the ensuing gifts and celebration on Christmas Eve to the solemnity of the Day of the Dead, Haitians find time and space to give thanks for what they have and honor those who paved the way for the lives they are able to live.

A people living so close to the edge of misfortune, as poor Haitians are, usually cannot afford one extra straw added to their burden. In 2010, they received more than they could bear. A 7.0 magnitude earthquake devastated the capital of Port-au-Prince, killing up to 160,000 people, and greatly disrupting the lives of nearly three million others. Ten months after that catastrophe, a cholera epidemic killed another nine thousand people and

Friends walk through the rubble of fallen buildings in Port-au-Prince months after the earthquake.

sickened more than 700,000. Exacerbated by Hurricane Sandy in 2012, the cholera outbreak was still not under control in 2015. Ironically and regrettably, the cholera is thought to have been brought into the already ravaged country by peacekeeping forces from Nepal. Regardless of its origin (Haiti had never before suffered an outbreak of cholera), the disease spread like wildfire through the unsanitary camps that lacked clean water.

In the years since the dual disasters, international relief aid and the work of the Haitian people and government have made some progress—but not nearly enough. Much work remains to be done, as has seemingly been the case since Haiti's independence in 1804.

With a history of political corruption and violence among the country's leadership, it is little wonder that Haitians are wary of their government. Since the 1957 election of François Duvalier, there has been a succession of—to put it mildly—problematic leaders, many using intimidation and violence to quell any popular dissent and quiet any criticism. Most of Haiti's leaders have exhibited no interest in aiding the country, preferring to use its limited resources to line their own pockets and increase their own power. Even the extremely popular former president Jean-Bertrand Aristide has been accused of corruption.

Many Haitians, therefore, have withdrawn from the electoral sphere, worried that any support they might show could be dangerous at best and deadly at worst. The current president, former pop star Michel Martelly, elected in 2011, is a known supporter of the highly corrupt and violent Duvalier regime. Since becoming president, Martelly has announced his desire to reinstate the military and do away with parliament. He has consistently postponed legislative elections and has been accused of accepting millions of dollars in bribes. Critics say the president has surrounded himself with a network of friends and associates, many of whom have been arrested or the focus of criminal investigations. Martelly's term will end in 2016 and he is not allowed to run again because the Haitian constitution does not allow for consecutive presidential terms. He could, however, run again in 2020.

President Michel Martelly gives a speech on the anniversary of the War for Haitian Independence in November 2013.

To be Haitian is to understand extremes. Their country remains one of the world's poorest in economic terms but one of its richest in cultural heritage. Haitian art and food reflect the country's French, Caribbean, and African influences, while the dominant religion, vodou, is the result of generations of slaves preserving their African beliefs under the guise of Catholicism. The national language of Haiti, Creole, is similarly a mixture of French and West African languages. For all of their cultural wealth, Haitians have suffered almost constantly from oppressive regimes, foreign invasions, and internal strife since Christopher Columbus landed on the island more than five hundred years ago. It is remarkable that even as disorder continues to plague the nation, Haitians carry on with great resilience.

GEOGRAPHY

The red hibiscus is the national flower of Haiti.

1

C OVERING A TOTAL AREA OF
10,714 square miles (27,750 square
kilometers)—an area slightly larger
than the state of Maryland, the Republic
of Haiti comprises the western third of the
island of Hispaniola, the second largest
island in the Caribbean. The rest of the
island is the Dominican Republic.

Haiti is shaped like a lobster claw. Its relationship with its island mate, the Dominican
Republic, is not especially good.

Haiti has numerous smaller islands. Of these, *Île de la Tortue* (Turtle Island) was a pirate stronghold in the seventeenth century. *Île à Vache* (Cow Island) is so named because it was once overrun by wild cows descended from animals abandoned by the Spanish.

Mountains are visible on the horizon in many parts of Haiti.

Haiti consists of a northern and southern peninsula separated by the Gulf of Gonâve. The shape of Haiti has been compared to a lobster's claw with the upper pincer pointing toward Cuba, the lower toward Jamaica. The landscape is characterized by broad bands of towering mountain ranges, interspersed with fertile lowland plains and lakes. Its location and topography predispose the island to frequent natural disasters, such as earthquakes, landslides, and tropical storms. Natural resources in Haiti are limited. Most of its forests have been denuded, its bauxite mining industry has collapsed, and the search for oil has been unsuccessful.

Together with Cuba, Puerto Rico, and Jamaica, Hispaniola forms the Greater Antilles, one of the four island chains that make up the West Indies. Lying 565 miles (909 km) southeast of Florida, Hispaniola is separated from Puerto Rico in the east by the Mona Passage and from Cuba in the west by the Windward Passage. These two passages are the principal maritime routes linking North America and Europe with South and Central America.

MOUNTAIN RANGES AND PLAINS

The word Haiti means "mountainous land" in the language of the Taíno Arawak, who were the first inhabitants of the island. The country is dominated by mountain ranges; more than three-quarters of the land area is highlands. Less than 20 percent of the land lies below 600 feet (183 meters), while 40 percent rises above 1,500 feet (457 m).

The longest mountain range, the Massif du Nord, runs southeast from the Atlantic coast and crosses the border with the Dominican Republic, where it becomes the Cordillera Central. Haiti's highest peak is La Selle, which at 8,793 feet (2,681 m) dominates the Massif de la Selle.

The Central Plain extends over 840 square miles (2,175 square km) from the Montagnes Noires to the border with the Dominican Republic. The North

PUSHING THE BORDER

Haiti's 193-mile (311-km) border with the Dominican Republic follows mountain ridges and streams from the north to the south of the island. Along a stretch of the interior highlands, the frontier is defined by the international route, a highway running parallel to the Libón River.

The valleys provide easy access between the island's two countries, with the result that the migration of Haitians to the Dominican Republic was always high. Haitian farmers suffering from a lack of land at home have always looked longingly at the vast, empty stretches of land beyond the border. By settling on parts of that land and claiming them for Haiti, they pushed the border farther into the Dominican Republic.

Haiti's brown, deforested landscape contrasts sharply with the green forests of its neighbor on the Haiti-Dominican Republic border.

When the practice became widespread, the Haitian government stepped in and tried to reinstate the original border, but the presence of military guards did not halt the flow of Haitians into the Dominican Republic. In 2015, a Dominican court ruling stripped citizenship from children born in the Dominican Republic of Haitian parents. The Dominican government then began deporting Haitian immigrants, and tens of thousands of people now live in refugee camps just across the border in Haiti. The deportation crisis is ongoing, with neither country accepting responsibility for the deported immigrants.

Roads are clearly visible on the denuded mountains.

Plain covers 150 square miles (389 square km) between the Massif du Nord and the Atlantic Ocean. This area, with its fertile soil, was the plantation heartland during the colonial period. Two smaller plains, the Artibonite and the Cul-de-Sac, border the Gulf of Gonâve.

Every inch of arable land is cultivated, and even very steep mountain slopes are tilled. Numerous stories have been told of farmers falling to their deaths from their cornfields. Much of Haiti suffers from extensive erosion due to overcultivation, and a muddy brown ring surrounds the country's coastline where the topsoil has washed into the sea.

TROPICAL FLORA

A few hundred years ago Haiti was covered with marshes of wild ginger, plantations of bananas and Indian corn, and tropical rain forests of mahogany, redwood, and pine. Now the landscape looks quite different. The plantations were subdivided after independence, while the vast expanses

14 Haiti

of trees gradually disappeared as more and more land was cleared to provide agricultural land for an ever-increasing population. Haiti is one of the few countries in the world where the destruction of the original woodland is almost complete. Surviving pine and hardwood trees now grow only on the upper levels of the mountains. Mangroves fringe the Gulf of Gonâve and the Atlantic Coast to the east of Cap Haïtien. Elsewhere along the coastline, thickets of guava fruit grow in profusion. The North Plain supports scattered patches of desert-like growth. Here, trees grow only along the edges of rivers and streams. In the northwestern reaches of the Central Plain, the grasslands are dotted with semideciduous trees and conifers, while the southeastern part is covered with scrub woodland and cacti. In the Artibonite Plain thorny scrub woodland near the coast gives way to grassland savannah and mixed woodland farther inland.

Tropical flowers, such as wild orchids, royal poincianas, bougainvilleas, poinsettias, and frangipani, provide stunning color, beauty, and fragrance. Native fruit trees include avocado, orange, lime, and cherry. About twenty species of plants that grow indigenously are useful for their nutritional or medicinal properties.

FAUNA

Indigenous to Haiti are several types of reptiles, including three varieties of crocodile, the rhino-horned iguana, small lizards, and non-poisonous snakes. Insects abound, as well as spiders, scorpions, and centipedes. Some of these insects can be poisonous, but their stings are rarely fatal.

As recently as the 1960s Haiti was a bird-lover's paradise. Spotted sandpipers, roseate flamingos, long-billed curlews, peregrine falcons, and black-bellied plovers all flourished. Deforestation has destroyed the habitats of many of these species, but parrots, wild pigeons, guinea hens, ducks, and weaver birds can still be found. Egrets and flamingos make their nests around the brackish lakes of the Cul-de-Sac plain.

The waters along the coast of Haiti and the country's numerous rivers support various species of fish. There are 270 species of fish in the coastal waters, including tarpon, kingfish, barracuda, and red snapper.

CLIMATE

Port-au-Prince is surrounded by mountains.

Haiti's climate is hot and dry all year. Temperatures vary slightly with elevation. The annual average is 81° Fahrenheit (27° Celsius) in the lowlands and 76°F (24°C) in the highlands. On the coast, sea breezes temper the heat. The hottest months are June to September and the coolest from February to April.

The mountains surrounding valleys form protective walls that, coupled with direct sunlight, can produce Haiti's highest temperatures. Haiti's capital, Port-au-Prince, is sheltered by mountains to the north and south. It is one of the hottest cities in the region.

Haiti lies in a rain shadow and generally receives less rainfall than its neighbor, the Dominican Republic. Rainfall produced by trade winds is stopped by the mountain ridge dividing the two countries. The north receives the most rain—20 to 100 inches (51 to 254 cm) per year—but the high rate of evaporation prevents most of the water from seeping into the soil. June through October is hurricane season in Haiti. Hurricanes often cause dangerous floods in the mountainous terrain. In 2004 Tropical Storm Jeanne killed nearly three thousand people around Gonaïves.

RIVERS AND LAKES

More than a hundred rivers and streams flow from the mountains into the sea. Although most Haitian rivers are shallow and unnavigable due to the high rate of evaporation, they are important for irrigation and the production of hydroelectricity.

The longest river in Haiti is the Artibonite River, which is about ten times longer than any of the others in the country. Originating in the Cordillera

Central in the Dominican Republic, the Artibonite flows 174 miles (280 km) west across Haiti before emptying into the Gulf of Gonâve. The damming of the upper Artibonite has produced Lake Péligre, a reservoir used for flood control, irrigation, and hydroelectricity.

The largest natural lake in Haiti is Étang Saumâtre with an area of 65 square miles (168 square km). It is home to many exotic species of wildlife.

CITIES AND TOWNS

PORT-AU-PRINCE The capital of Haiti was founded in 1749 and has been rebuilt several times after earthquakes (the most recent in 2010) and fires. The streets of Port-au-Prince reveal the extreme contrasts between rich and poor that are characteristic of Haiti: dirty, dusty, and overcrowded shantytowns stand side by side with elegant mansions and gleaming public buildings. Port-au-Prince has expanded in recent years to absorb neighboring towns and an influx of economic refugees from the countryside and other cities. It is Haiti's largest urban area with more than three million residents.

CAP-HAÏTIEN Also called Le Cap, this city was once the capital of the French colony of Saint-Domingue and was known as Little Paris. After independence King Henri Christophe made it his capital. Today, it is the second-largest city with approximately 190,300 inhabitants.

INTERNET LINKS

traveltips.usatoday.com/famous-landforms-haiti-59326.html
This is a quick listing of important geographic landforms in Haiti.

www.wunderground.com/resources/education/haiti.asp
"Hurricanes and Haiti: A Tragic History" looks at the country's experiences with natural disasters.

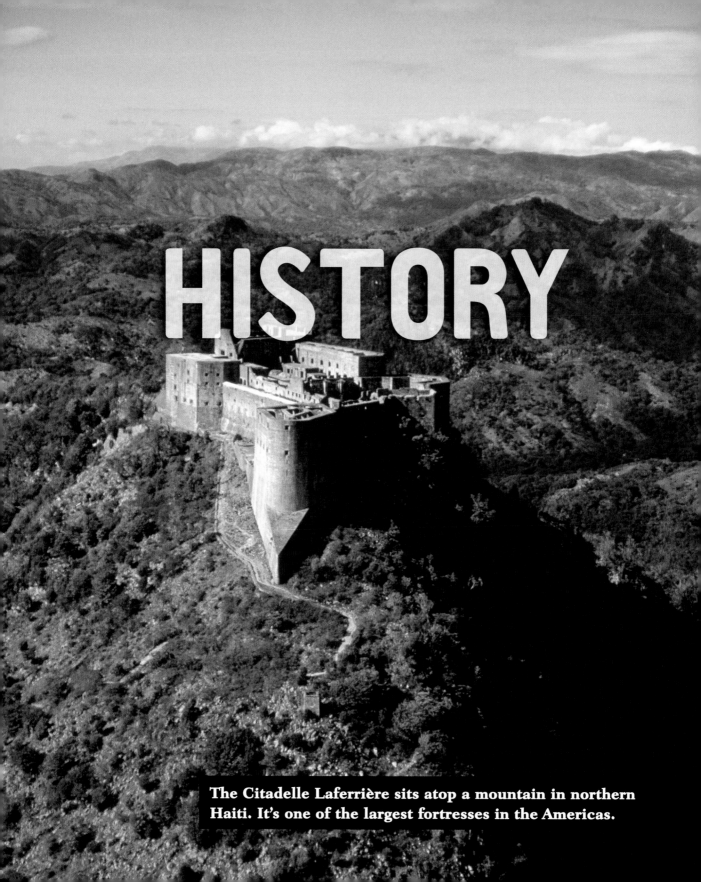

HISTORY

The Citadelle Laferrière sits atop a mountain in northern Haiti. It's one of the largest fortresses in the Americas.

2

AFTER A SLAVE REVOLT IN 1791 against their French colonizers, Haiti became the first black independent republic in the world in 1804. Despite this remarkably early liberation and a bold national motto—"Strength Through Union"—Haiti has endured a tumultuous history characterized by enormous struggle and bloodshed. After almost two hundred years of rule by a series of despotic emperors, eccentric kings, cruel dictators, weak presidents, and tyrannical generals, nothing has really improved for average Haitians. Today they still face severe economic and social problems while they struggle to establish and maintain a stable democratic government.

In the eighteenth century, under French rule, Haiti—then called Saint-Domingue—was called "the Pearl of the Antilles," and was one of the richest islands in the Caribbean. However, that wealth was produced and supported by the labor of some 500,000 to 800,000 African slaves, who far outnumbered the white and mixed-race people.

BEFORE COLUMBUS

The island of Hispaniola was inhabited from around 5000 BCE by Paleo-Indians, a group of hunter-gatherers who are believed to have come from Central America. In 1000 BCE Meso-Indians, hunter-gatherers who also knew how to make tools and pottery, spread from South America to the Greater Antilles. When Christopher Columbus arrived in the fifteenth century, Hispaniola was inhabited by a gentle and peace-loving people of native Arawak descent, who called themselves Taíno Arawak, or "The Good People."

Columbus lands on Hispaniola and is greeted by Arawak people on December 6, 1492.

HISPANIOLA

Christopher Columbus "discovered" Hispaniola on his first voyage to the Americas in 1492. It was one of the first islands he encountered, and he named it *La Isla Española* (or the Spanish Island, later anglicized to Hispan-iola) and claimed it for the kingdom of Spain. The Taíno Arawak he met were friendly and offered gold ornaments to him and his crew. This led Columbus to believe that the island was rich in gold. When Columbus returned to Europe, he left some men on Hispaniola with orders to look for gold.

The Spaniards left on the island, however, soon offended the indigenous people, and when Columbus returned to Haiti on his second expedition to the New World, he found his men killed and the fort they built destroyed. Columbus instituted a system that forced the Taíno Arawak into servitude for the Spanish. Columbus also established a new settlement on the south coast of the island, in what is now the Dominican Republic. This settlement was the first permanent European colony in the Americas, and the Spaniards named it Santo Domingo. Subsequently, more settlers arrived from Spain

BUCCANEERS

In the first half of the seventeenth century, a group of French and English buccaneers took refuge on Tortuga Island after being driven off the Caribbean island of St. Christopher by the Spanish. The small community was soon joined by Dutch refugees. The early buccaneers were escaped servants, former soldiers, and logwood cutters from what is now southern Mexico. Together, they hunted wild boar and cattle, and cultivated crops.

Buccaneers acquired their name from their custom of curing meat on spits called boucans (boo-CAHN). Each nationality also had its own term for the adventurers—the French called them flibustiers *(flih-buhss-TEEAY, from the Dutch word for "freebooter"), the Dutch* zeerovers *(see-ROH-vehrs, or sea rovers), and the Spanish* corsarios *(kohr-SAH-riohs). Their stories inspired such authors as Jonathan Swift, Daniel Defoe, and Robert Louis Stevenson.*

To combat attacks by the Spaniards, the buccaneers banded together and called themselves the Brethren of the Coast. The more aggressive ones engaged in piracy against Spanish ships. Tortuga Island, 10 miles (16 km) out to sea from Port-de-Paix on the northern coast of Haiti, was an ideal launching pad for attacks on Spanish ships transporting gold between Central America and Europe. The buccaneers worked in small crews and became known for their extreme cruelty. England, France, and the Netherlands did nothing to prevent the attacks, as they were eager to break Spain's trade monopoly. Buccaneering finally came to an end toward the end of the seventeenth century.

and were granted large tracts of land to use as they pleased. They established sugar plantations and made the Taíno Arawak work in them. Hard labor and European diseases took their toll on the Taíno Arawak, and by the mid-sixteenth century the native population had declined from one million to five thousand. The labor shortage became acute, so the settlers began to ship large numbers of slaves to Haiti from Africa. By 1520 almost all laborers on Hispaniola were African slaves. In 1535 Hispaniola became part of the Viceroyalty of New Spain. The Spanish also used Hispaniola as a base for exploring the region. But when large quantities of gold were discovered in Mexico and Peru, Santo Domingo's importance was overshadowed, and Spain lost interest in Hispaniola.

THE FRENCH COLONY OF SAINT-DOMINGUE

In 1625 English and French buccaneers established a base on Tortuga Island off the northern coast of Haiti to launch their attacks on the gold-laden Spanish galleons sailing from Central America to Europe. Sixteen years later, the buccaneers moved to the mainland and founded the settlement of Port Margot on the northwestern tip of the island. Soon after, the French drove out the English and renamed the territory Saint-Domingue.

The French concentrated on two extremely profitable activities, farming and piracy, and Saint-Domingue quickly prospered. In 1697 the Spanish ceded the western third of Hispaniola to France under the Treaty of Ryswick, while retaining control of the eastern two-thirds.

The French colonists successfully grew sugarcane, coffee, cocoa, cotton, and indigo on vast plantations worked by half a million African slaves. A fleet of seven hundred ships carrying annual exports worth $40 million sailed between Saint-Domingue and Europe. Saint-Domingue was soon the most profitable slave colony in the world, contributing to much of the wealth of major French ports, such as Marseille.

Saint-Domingue's plantation owners, known as *grands blancs* (grahn BLAHN), literally "great white men," also acquired enormous wealth and lived in such luxury that they became the envy of all of Europe. The capital of the colony, Cap Français, was regarded as the Paris of the New World.

By this time, several thousand mulatto *affranchis* (ah-frahn-SHEE), or "freemen," had also become the owners of large sugar plantations. Affranchis were Haitians of mixed African and European descent, who had won their freedom from slavery and had been granted French citizenship. Despite the affranchis' considerable wealth, the white planters did not regard or treat them as equals, and consequently, hostilities between the two groups increased.

A major battle of the Haitian Revolution is illustrated in this painting by Auguste Raffet—the Battle of Crête-à-Pierrot in 1802.

THE FIRST BLACK REPUBLIC

In 1789 the French Revolution's proclamation of "equality among all men," led the affranchis to push for their own equality with the white planters in Saint-Domingue. A mulatto demonstration in 1791 resulted in riots and a major slave rebellion. The rebellion was led by François Dominique Toussaint, who

"Hidden God in a cloud
  is there, watching us.
  He sees all the whites do;
  the White god demands crimes
  ours wants good things.
  But our God that is so good
  orders vengeance, he will
  ride us, assist us.
  Throw away the thoughts of
  the White god who thirsts
  for our tears, listen to
  freedom that speaks from our hearts."

With this invocation at a vodou ceremony at Bois-Caiman on August 14, 1791, Jamaican-born Boukman Dutty, a vodou priest, urged his countrymen to rise up in arms. One week later, fifty thousand insurgents seized control of the important North Plain for ten days.

White planters were killed and the sugar plantations destroyed. Uprisings broke out across the country. By the time Haiti declared independence in 1804, one hundred thousand Haitians were dead.

was also known as Toussaint Louverture. He was a former slave, a grandson of an African chieftain, and a first-class military strategist with considerable leadership qualities who quickly moved up the ranks of the French army. As a result of the rebellion, slavery was abolished in Saint-Domingue in 1793.

Spanish and British invaders attempted to take control of the sugar plantations that were destroyed during the slave revolt, but Toussaint and his army successfully repelled the foreign forces. Meanwhile, Santo Domingo, the eastern two-thirds of Hispaniola, failed to flourish under Spanish rule, and in 1795 Spain ceded their share of the island to France under the Treaty of Basle.

In 1801 Toussaint appointed himself governor-for-life of both Saint-Domingue and Santo Domingo, but it was independence from France and the abolition of slavery that he truly desired. Toussaint freed the slaves in Santo Domingo but stopped short of declaring the independence of Hispaniola.

Napoleon, intent on expanding his empire, was not prepared to lose such a valuable slave colony. He sent a huge army and fleet of ships to Hispaniola to overthrow Toussaint and restore slavery in Santo Domingo. Napoleon's army did succeed in capturing Toussaint, shipping him off to France as a prisoner, but they underestimated the strength and fervor of Haitian nationalist forces led by army generals Henri Christophe, Jean-Jacques Dessalines, and Alexandre Pétion. Yellow fever contributed to the downfall of the French, and they surrendered to Dessalines in 1803.

On January 1, 1804, Dessalines proclaimed the independence of Saint-Domingue. The first black republic in the world was renamed Haiti.

EMPERORS AND KINGS

After independence, General Jean-Jacques Dessalines proclaimed himself Jean-Jacques the First, Emperor of Haiti. He was a cruel leader who ordered the execution of most of the whites still in Haiti. He was assassinated in 1806, and it was then that civil war broke out between mulattoes, led by Alexandre Pétion, and blacks, led by Henri Christophe. Christophe took control of the north, crowned himself King of Haiti, and set about building palaces and fortresses. He suffered a stroke in 1820 and committed suicide soon after. Pétion was president of the south until his death in 1818. The country was

François Dominique Toussaint was born in 1743. He got his nickname Louverture *(loo-vair-TOOR, or "the opening") in the days of the rebellion. Some say the name comes from the fact that he opened the way to freedom for the black people, while others say it was because he was so good at opening moves in battle. Still others believe that it referred to the wide gap between his two front teeth.*

Although Toussaint was a slave, his master allowed him to learn to read and write, and even to borrow his books. As a child, he had to work in the fields together with the other slaves. His reading and conversations with the other slaves gave him knowledge of other lands where people were free and happy. Toussaint was a man of superior intellect; he learned the secrets of medicinal herbs and plants and how to treat sick people with them. He was soon well-known among the slaves.

When Toussaint was in his forties, the slave revolt broke out, and he decided to join the insurgents. As one of the few slaves who could read and write, he was a natural choice to be the leader. Toussaint had never been to military school, but his reading had given him a great knowledge of military tactics. He always made careful plans, taking his enemies by surprise and outmaneuvering them.

In 1793 France agreed to free the slaves in Saint-Domingue, although it was to remain a French colony. Toussaint then became a general in the French army, fighting against the

British and the Spanish, who were attacking Saint-Domingue by land and sea. In 1801 he declared himself governor-for-life. Napoleon, who came to power in France in 1799, refused to recognize the abolition of slavery in Santo Domingo and sent a large army to fight the newly emancipated slaves.

After a few months of resistance, Toussaint was tricked into boarding a French boat, where he was arrested. He was taken to France and thrown into a medieval castle prison high in the mountains near the Swiss border. He died of pneumonia there two years later. When he was deported from Haiti, Toussaint vowed that the struggle for freedom would continue: "In overthrowing me, they have cut down in Saint-Domingue the trunk of the tree of black liberty. It will shoot up again through the roots, for they are numerous and deep."

then reunited in 1820 under President Jean-Pierre Boyer, who governed until 1843. Unrest and turmoil soon began again, however, and Haiti saw twenty-two successive heads of state in the next seventy-two years. Most of these leaders were forced out of office by violent means.

THE US OCCUPATION

In 1915 the United States invaded Haiti on the pretext that the political instability there was a danger to US security in the region. Four Haitian presidents had been killed or deposed in as many years, but the real trigger for the invasion was a Haitian law that prevented foreign ownership of Haitian land or businesses. This was a direct threat to US business interests.

Many Haitians were opposed to the military occupation. The Haitians who took up arms against the US forces were met with force. Thousands of Haitians died in their rebellion against the United States. The United States did, however, build much-needed infrastructure and medical facilities but forced Haitians to work, unpaid, in some of their construction. When the Marines withdrew in 1934, Americans controlled Haiti's central bank, railway, sugar refineries, and power stations. They also left behind a new Haitian Army that would become the scourge of the population for sixty years. The United States continued to control Haiti's finances until 1947.

THE DUVALIER YEARS

When the Americans left, Haiti was again in turmoil and witnessed frequent coups, revolutions, dictatorships, and street violence, until the election of François Duvalier in 1957. Duvalier, a conservative black doctor and student of vodou, promised to restore power to the blacks. He was hailed as a liberator and affectionately called Papa Doc.

Papa Doc's rule soon turned into one of repression and fear. With the help of his personal and brutal police force, the Tontons Macoute, he created an environment that kept the Haitian people in a constant state of terror. Papa Doc was a fanatical dictator and became known as "Lucifer of the Antilles." Haiti was shunned by the rest of the world,

and many of the country's educated and wealthy mulattoes emigrated.

Although originally elected for a term of six years, Papa Doc declared himself president-for-life in 1964. In 1971, just before he died, he changed the constitution to enable him to designate his nineteen-year-old son Jean-Claude, or Baby Doc, as his successor.

Baby Doc eased the repression just enough to gain international respectability and the restoration of US aid. Despite this and a short-term revival of the tourist industry during the 1970s, Haiti's economy stagnated. While Baby Doc and his wealthy mulatto wife, Michèle Bennett, lived an extravagant lifestyle in the National Palace, most of the Haitian people slipped deeper and deeper into poverty. Thousands of Haitians from all walks of life fled the country in search of a better life.

Hostility toward the excesses of the Duvalier regime and the worsening poverty increased during the early 1980s. In 1985, sixty thousand youths demonstrated with the rallying cry, "We would rather die on our feet than live on our knees." Despite a full show of force by the Tontons Macoute, Jean-Claude Duvalier and his family were forced to leave Haiti in 1986. They were flown to France by the US military.

President François "Papa Doc" Duvalier is shown in a formal portrait in 1965.

ATTEMPTS AT DEMOCRACY

After the ousting of Jean-Claude Duvalier, a National Council of Government was established under the army chief, Lieutenant General Henri Namphy. Although the council dissolved the pro-Duvalier legislature and—officially, at least—disbanded the Tontons Macoute, it could not cope with the ensuing political and economic chaos. A new constitution was approved in March 1987, providing for a president, a prime minister, and a two-chamber legislature. On Election Day in November 1987, troops opened fire on citizens who were lined up to vote, killing between thirty and three hundred people, according to conflicting reports. Military leaders canceled the election and retained control of the government. Finally, the first elections in nearly three decades were held in 1988, but there were allegations of widespread fraud, and less than 10 percent of Haitians turned out to vote. The man who was elected president, Leslie Manigat, lasted only three months before he too was ousted by the military.

After several coups d'état, the Haitian population again went to the polls in December 1990. To the great jubilation of the Haitian people, Jean-Bertrand Aristide, a left-wing Roman Catholic priest, was elected with 67 percent of the vote. He lost no time in implementing land reform, combating illiteracy, controlling the army, and shrinking the bureaucracy, but these actions alienated the upper class and the army. In an army-led revolt in September 1991, Aristide was abducted and deported to Venezuela. A military government took control under the direction of Lieutenant General Raoul Cédras. The international community quickly responded by cutting off aid and imposing a trade embargo.

Former President Jean-Bertrand Aristide returns to Haiti in 2011.

ARISTIDE RETURNS—AND LEAVES AGAIN

In 1994, a deal was brokered by former US president Jimmy Carter. It allowed Aristide to return to power in Haiti but granted full immunity to the military for the thousands of murders it committed. Aristide was also forced to adopt harsh economic reforms and slow down his campaign to alleviate poverty. He was prevented by the constitution from running for re-election in 1995, but his colleague, René Préval, won. In 2000, Aristide was again elected by a wide majority, but this time there were allegations of electoral fraud.

During the winter of 1991–1992, owing to the violence against the supporters of ousted President Aristide, nearly forty thousand people tried to escape from Haiti by boat, heading for the United States. Those that didn't die during the 600-mile (965.6 kilometers)

trip were picked up by the US Coast Guard and detained in Cuba. Eventually the number of refugees got to be too much, and President George H. W. Bush ordered all boat people returned to Haiti, regardless of whether or not they qualified for asylum. When Bill Clinton was elected president, he continued the policy and worked to restore

Aristide to office in 1994, claiming that by refusing Haitian refugees, the United States could help prevent more Haitian deaths from drowning. Though the policy might have prevented further drownings, Clinton's return of political refugees and Aristide's restoration to the presidency did nothing to fix the ongoing political issues rife within Haiti.

Haiti's elite also continued to oppose the people's government, sponsoring violence and gang warfare in the shantytowns. On February 29, 2004, Aristide was forced into exile following a coup d'état. Some, including Aristide himself, say the United States played a secret role in his removal. He spent his years away in the Central African Republic and then South Africa, where he remained until his return in 2011.

An interim government headed by Boniface Alexandre and backed by a US military presence was installed. In 2011, Michel Martelly was more or less peacefully elected president.

TRAGEDY SHAKES THE EARTH

In January 2010, a massive 7.0-magnitude earthquake struck Haiti. The earthquake killed more than 160,000 people and left nearly 1.5 million people without homes. The epicentre was just outside the capital city of Port-Au-Prince. Even five years later, many half-destroyed buildings remained untouched all over the capital. Despite billions of dollars pledged in international aid, many Haitians remain homeless and do not have access to adequate medical care. Many people in the country are worse off today, socially and economically, than they were before the earthquake.

INTERNET LINKS

www.cnn.com/2013/07/18/world/jean-bertrand-aristide-fast-facts
Here are fast facts and a timeline about Jean-Bertrand Aristide.

www.miamiherald.com/news/nation-world/world/americas/haiti/article1984677.html
A news story explains a 2015 investigation into the alleged crimes of former President Aristide.

www.npr.org/sections/goatsandsoda/2015/01/12/376138864/5-years-after-haiti-s-earthquake-why-aren-t-things-better
This NPR story asks why so much humanitarian aid has not done more to improve life in Haiti.

www.theguardian.com/world/2010/jan/14/haiti-history-earthquake-disaster
"Haiti: A Long Descent to Hell" asks why Haiti suffers so much misery.

www.usnews.com/news/photos/2015/01/09/photos-haitis-recovery-5-years-after-devastating-earthquake
This is an excellent slide show of images of Haiti five years after the earthquake.

GOVERNMENT

The National Palace, also known as the Presidential Palace, no longer stands in Port-au-Prince.

3

HOPES WERE HIGH WHEN HAITI emancipated itself from the French in 1804. It was, after all, the first free nation whose population had a black majority. Sadly, the optimism that accompanied Haiti's post-colonial history was short-lived. Even after nearly two centuries of independence, the Haitian people are still struggling to achieve true democracy. Its constitution, originally based on the French Napoleonic Code and the US Constitution, has been changed many times over the years, mainly to reinforce the positions of those in power. Virtual dictatorship has been the rule for the almost fifty years since François Duvalier declared himself president-for-life.

After the collapse of the Duvalier regimes, Haitian politics were marked by a period of coups d'état, rigged elections, and martial law. Since then, Haiti has experienced a number of democratic elections, but

In 2014, the Corruption Perceptions Index rated Haiti number 161 out of 175 countries with a score of 19, on a scale from 0 to 100, where 0 is "highly corrupt" and 100 is "very clean." This index, compiled annually by Transparency International, defines corruption as "the misuse of public power for private benefit."

The prime minister of Haiti, Evans Paul, speaks to the media in 2015.

every elected government has faced the implacable challenge of serving a deeply divided country.

NATIONAL GOVERNMENT

The present Haitian constitution, adopted in March 1987, declares that Haiti is a republic with three branches of government: executive, legislative, and judicial.

THE EXECUTIVE Executive power is shared by the president of the republic, who is directly elected for a term of five years, and the prime minister, who is chosen by the president with the approval of the National Assembly. The president is the head of state and is barred from serving consecutive terms. The prime minister is the head of government.

THE LEGISLATURE The Haitian National Assembly, like the US Congress, is made up of two houses: the thirty-seat Senate and the ninety-nine-seat Chamber of Deputies. Members of both houses are elected by a national vote; the senators for a term of six years, and the deputies for four-year terms.

THE JUDICIARY Haitian law is based on the French Napoleonic Code, with certain modifications made by the Duvalier regime. The judicial system has four levels: the Court of Cassation, the Court of Appeal, civil courts, and magistrates' courts. The Court of Cassation is similar to the US Supreme Court, and judges for both the Court of Cassation and the Court of Appeal are appointed by the president for a period of ten years, (even though the Haitian Constitution states "Judges of the Supreme Court are appointed for life"). They may not be removed from office unless found guilty of misconduct. Judges for the other courts serve for seven years.

The elegant, gleaming white building served as the home of Haitian presidents. It was located in Port-au-Prince, facing Place L'Overture near the Champs de Mars. Built in 1914–1920, in the French Renaissance style, the palace was more than twice the size of the White House in Washington, DC.

When the earthquake hit Port-au-Prince in 2010, the National Palace was severely damaged and could no longer be occupied. Its collapsed cupola, the center dome, became a symbol of the devastated nation. In 2012, the building was razed, and despite promises to rebuild, no real plans yet exist.

LOCAL GOVERNMENT

Haiti is divided geographically into nine sections called departments that are responsible for the administration of local government. The nine departments are further divided into about a hundred communes. Each department has its own capital, and each commune has a *bourg* (BOOR), a major town with municipal authority, and five or six sections *rurales* (sec-SIOHN ruh-RAHL), or "rural districts." The *rurales* are administered by local district leaders appointed by the government.

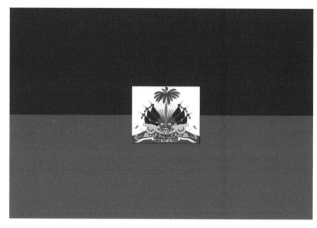

During colonial days the Haitian flag was the same as the French flag, consisting of three vertical bands: blue, white, and red. During the Haitian War of Independence, in the city of Arcahaie on May 18, 1803, rebel leader Jean-Jacques Dessalines ripped out the white part of the flag as a symbol of the Haitians' hatred for the white colonizers. In 1818 Jean-Pierre Boyer adopted a new pattern of blue and red horizontal bands and a coat of arms, but François Duvalier changed the bands to vertical black and red in 1964. At the end of the Duvalier regime in 1986, the pre-Duvalier flag of horizontal bands in blue and red was reintroduced. The coat of arms is positioned against a white background in the center of the flag.

CONSTITUTIONAL REFORM

The 1987 constitution includes many provisions intended to safeguard the democratic rights of the Haitian people. It provides for:

- the equality of all Haitians before the law,
- full political rights, including voting rights, for all Haitians above age twenty-one,
- freedom of the press and freedom of thought,
- the recognition of Creole as an official language,
- the right to practice religions and faiths freely,
- the separation of the military and the police,
- an independent electoral commission,
- an independent judiciary,
- the abolition of the death penalty,
- a ten-year ban on Duvalier regime officials from holding office.

In reality, however, many of these reforms have failed to materialize, and the constitution has been partially or fully suspended several times since it came into effect.

UNCERTAIN DEMOCRACY

In the three open elections since the downfall of Jean-Claude Duvalier (1951–2014) in 1986 (1990, 1995, 2000), the Haitian majority has chosen candidates promising to reform the government and economy in favor of the poor. This is not surprising in a country where 80 percent of the population lives in poverty. While Aristide was able to make a few important changes, such as disbanding the Armed Forces in 1995, he was not effective in alleviating poverty. Both he and René Préval (Aristide's successor) faced an inflexible Haitian business class and criticism from abroad for their policies.

Aristide resigned, left the country in 2004 to live in exile in South Africa. He returned in 2011, but has not sought a return to politics. At the time of Aristide's resignation, Chief Justice Boniface Alexandre became interim president. The current president (as of August 2015), Michel Martelly is associated with Duvalier, continuing the troubling history of corruption and distrust associated with Haitians' attempts at true democracy.

INTERNET LINKS

af.reuters.com/article/topNews/idAFJOE72I01L20110319
This article from 2011, "Aristide Makes Triumphant Haiti Return Before Vote" highlights Aristide's popularity in Haiti.

www.cia.gov/library/publications/the-world-factbook/geos/ha.html
The CIA World Factbook gives up-to-date information about Haiti's government.

www.transparency.org/research/cpi/overview
This is the home of the Corruption Perceptions Index.

ECONOMY

A young man loads his boat with wood to transport to the nation's capital 177 miles (286 km) away.

HAITI HAS NOT FAIRED WELL IN the modern world economy. Once the richest slave economy in the world, Haiti is now the poorest country in the Western Hemisphere and ranks 168 out of 187 countries on the 2014 UN Human Development Index. Haiti's economy has been overly reliant on the agricultural sector, leading to deforestation in an attempt to squeeze as much agriculture from every bit of arable land. In the last three decades, governments have tried diversifying into light manufacturing, where Haitians assemble goods destined for North America. These low-paying jobs have not alleviated poverty and are highly unstable, leaving workers with no job security. Increasing agricultural exports have also added to the risk of food shortages for the poor.

4

The United States is the largest donor of foreign aid to Haiti, followed by Canada and the European Union.

AGRICULTURE

Agriculture is the largest sector of the Haitian economy, accounting for
nearly a third of gross domestic product and employing more than two-
thirds of the population. Haitian agriculture is typified by small farms. After
independence, large estates were dismantled and redistributed in small plots
to thousands of black farmers. Plots are becoming smaller and smaller as
families subdivide their property among their children. Every square inch of
arable land is cultivated, and it is becoming increasingly difficult to get good
yields as erosion and overcultivation take their toll on the soil.

The main export crop is coffee, which is grown on Haiti's numerous
mountain slopes, but worldwide overproduction and a drop in prices have
led to a decrease in Haiti's export earnings. Sugar, which used to be the

The gourd (gourde in French), or calabash, is a very important vegetable to the poor Haitian farmer. Its flesh is used in many ways in Haitian cooking, and its shell, when dried, makes a versatile container, especially for carrying water. The leaves of the calabash tree (a type of creeper) can also be eaten. After becoming king of northern Haiti in 1807, Henri Christophe decreed that all calabash trees were the property of the state, and so all gourds had to be bought.

The use of the name gourde *for a unit of the Haitian currency has continued ever since. One gourde is divided into 100 centimes. During the US occupation and in the Duvalier years, the gourde was protected from devaluation by a convention signed with the United States. The exchange rate in 2015 with the US dollar was about 51 gourdes to one US dollar.*

backbone of the Haitian economy, has also declined in importance. Growing sugarcane requires large tracts of flat land and considerable amounts of rainfall, both of which are in short supply in Haiti. Most of the sugarcane grown on small farms is ground in rural distilleries to produce a type of rum called *clairin* (clay-REHN).

Most agricultural workers are engaged in the production of food crops for local consumption. The most important are the staples of the Haitian diet—rice, corn, and yams—and other vegetables and fruits, particularly mangoes. Haiti is also the world's leading supplier of vetiver, a root plant used in luxury perfumes.

MANUFACTURING

Manufacturing is the third most important sector of the economy after agriculture and commerce. Despite strong growth in the late 1970s, the manufacturing sector has shrunk in recent years due to Haiti's history of political instability and past international trade and oil embargoes. Foreign earnings from exports have dropped overall, but manufactured goods are still Haiti's primary export, followed by coffee, vegetable oils, and cocoa.

The main sources of manufacturing jobs are US-owned assembly plants around Port-au-Prince that produce clothing such as jeans and underwear. The manufacturing industry was initially established by Baby Doc, who lured companies with the promise of cheap and abundant labor, generous tax concessions, and an almost nonexistent trade union movement.

More recently, due to the climate of political instability and accusations of worker abuse, many companies have moved out of Haiti. In addition, manufacturing is also limited by the lack of regular electricity, waste disposal, and local consumers.

On the other hand, Haiti offers the lowest wage rates in the Western Hemisphere, so if the interim government builds the assembly plants, companies could still return to take advantage of Haiti's cheap labor and close proximity to the US market.

A woman works a sewing machine at a clothing manufacturer in Port-au-Prince in 2014.

Due in part to the high rates of unemployment and poverty, many Haitians do not use cash. Instead, they get their daily necessities through the nineteenth-century barter system. Usually farmers grow one or two types of vegetables, set aside what they need for themselves, and exchange the rest with other farmers for different kinds of vegetables or rice, or with shop owners for clothes and shoes. In order to buy the items that cannot be bartered, farmers sell some of their farm produce by the roadside for cash. In societies through which little cash moves, often barter is the most useful way for people with different strengths and needs to get the important things they need to survive.

THE WORK FORCE

The Haitian economy, concentrated in Port-au-Prince, has always employed only a small fraction of the 4.8 million-strong labor force. Some 38 percent of the employed labor force works in agriculture, around half in the service sector, and only 11 percent relies on industry jobs. Despite low wages, these workers might still be considered the lucky ones as the unemployment rate hovers at 40 percent (as of 2010). More than two-thirds of the labor force does not have formal employment.

The labor union movement was legally recognized for the first time in 1948, but growth has been quite slow because of the relatively small number of industrial workers and professionals compared to farmers and rural laborers. Moreover, workers seeking to unionize often face repression or lose their jobs when plant managers relocate to avoid dealing with union negotiators.

INTERNATIONAL EMBARGOES

When Aristide was ousted from power in 1991, the Organization of American States (OAS) imposed a trade embargo on Haiti. The embargo quickly led to food and fuel shortages, a sharp increase in food prices, and a drop in economic output. The assembly industries were badly hit with the majority of manufacturing plants being forced to close down since their supplies of raw materials were stopped, and there was no power to run machinery. An estimated sixty thousand jobs were lost. Ordinary Haitians suffered widespread malnutrition and faced famine, especially in rural areas. By the time the embargoes ended following the return to civilian rule in late 1994, the Haitian economy was already devastated.

TRANSPORTATION

In Port-au-Prince, one distinctive form of transportation is the *publique* (puh-BLIK), a shared taxi that picks up several passengers along the way. Everyone pays the same fare, regardless of the distance traveled, and the passenger going to the nearest destination is dropped off first. Publiques are easily recognizable by the red ribbon they display on their rearview mirror or radiator cap and the letter *P* on their license plate.

Busloads of people leave the capital city after the earthquake.

For rural travel, most people use *taptaps* (TAP-taps), Haiti's colorful public buses. However, the poor still travel long distances on foot, often without shoes. Small boats and ferries, though typically extremely slow and treacherously overloaded with people, animals, and cargo, are the most common method of transportation from one coastal village to another.

THE COST OF POLITICAL TURMOIL

As one of the poorest countries on earth, Haiti can ill afford any disruptions or setbacks in its economy. Sadly, it has experienced both in abundance. Lacking significant natural resources and run by an elite that views itself as unrelated and disconnected from the majority, Haiti has had little chance for development. Instability also dissuades Haitians with skills or money from staying or investing in Haiti. As they leave, all Haiti has left to offer is cheap, unskilled labor. With only poor paying jobs, there are few consumers for local products, causing the whole economy to spiral downward.

INTERNET LINKS

hdr.undp.org/en/countries/profiles/HTI
Haiti's Human Development report is available here, with a link to an explanatory pdf.

www.heritage.org/index/country/haiti
The 2015 Index of Economic Freedom ranks Haiti's economy.

www.usaid.gov/news-information/fact-sheets/us-assistance-haiti-overview-2010-2015-december-2014
This fact sheet details the accomplishments of US government aid to Haiti from 2010 to 2015.

www.worldbank.org/en/country/haiti/overview
The World Bank offers an overview of Haiti's political and economic situation.

ENVIRONMENT

Haiti president Michel Martelly, left, speaks with Dominican Republic president Danilo Medina about a reforestation program on World Environment Day 2013.

5

CENTURIES OF MISMANAGEMENT and exploitation have badly, perhaps irrevocably, damaged Haiti's natural environment. Crucially, Haiti has lost 98 percent of its natural forest cover and is losing what remains at a rate of 30 percent per year. Deforestation results in soil erosion, which leaches silt into the ocean and coral reefs, and destroys aquatic habitats. Without soil, the land cannot absorb rainfall, leaving Haiti water-poor as well. Commercial logging, international politics, and the poverty of the Haitian people have caused this disastrous situation. Left unaddressed, the consequences are dire for all living beings within Haiti. Solutions will only be found when the international community joins with Haitians in working to save their land.

Some fifty million trees are cut in Haiti each year to make charcoal. The production of charcoal takes place all over the country but the product is mostly sold in Port-au-Prince where the demand is greatest.

HAITI'S ASSETS

As a mountainous country, Haiti has rich biodiversity because each elevation above sea level has its own species of plants, birds, and animals. Haiti has more than five thousand species of plants alone, including six hundred varieties of ferns and three hundred types of orchids. There are hundreds of bird species that use the island as a stopover in their migrations between North and South America and twenty-five species that nest in Haiti. Tragically, there are almost no indigenous mammals left in Haiti due to over-hunting and destruction of their habitats.

HAITI'S FORESTS

When Columbus arrived in 1492, Haiti was covered in lush vegetation that extended up the mountainsides. By the early twentieth century, Haiti had lost 40 percent of its forests to commercial logging for tropical woods like mahogany. Since then, commercial logging has continued for the export market and to supply local craftspeople who make wood carvings for the

Along the road to Seguin, a mountain shows signs of erosion due to a lack of vegetation.

tourist market. Due to the trade embargoes and the end of fuel subsidies in the 1990s, demand for wood-based fuels has also soared, and many poor farmers have turned to charcoal-making to augment their meager earnings.

This aerial view shows soil erosion and flooding along the coast.

The loss of forests also means the loss of habitats for birds and animals, such as the Ridgway's hawk, plain pigeon, Ricord's iguana and Puerto Rican hutia. In the last century, forests and wildlife in Haiti have been sacrificed so that poor Haitians can survive.

A VICIOUS CYCLE

Most of Haiti, about 60 percent, is mountainous terrain. The steep hillsides and high elevations do not support farming and are susceptible to soil erosion if tree and plant cover are insufficient to anchor the soil in place.

With so few trees left, about 15,000 acres (6,070 hectares) of topsoil get washed into the ocean every year. This soil floats in the water as silt, which chokes corals and blocks sunlight to the ocean floor. In the process, fish habitats are destroyed and Haitian fishermen bring in smaller catches. As tree and plant roots also act as sponges when there is heavy rain, Haiti, with its denuded hillsides, is especially vulnerable during the annual storm season. Rather than being absorbed by the soil, rainwater flows directly into rivers, which then burst their banks, leading to flash floods.

Due to soil erosion, most of the damage caused by tropical storms is from the flash floods rather than from high winds. Floods not only cause serious damage to human settlements but also contaminate water sources, since they mix sewage water with drinking water. This contamination of the drinking water often leads to outbreaks of diseases, such as cholera and dysentery in the flood-affected areas, greatly increasing the human cost of these yearly events.

In the long term, soil erosion reduces the fertility of the land. This in turn, reduces crop yields and leaves poor farmers with insufficient food. Hungry Haitians are then forced to cut trees to make charcoal to sell as cooking fuel, completing a vicious cycle of environmental destruction and human tragedy.

A man in Titanyen, Haiti, cooks wood into charcoal inside a dirt mound.

INTERNATIONAL GEOPOLITICS

In order to force an illegal military government from power, Haiti's trade partners agreed to stop selling fuel to the government in 1991. The embargo lasted until 1994 when the democratically-elected president, Jean-Bertrand Aristide, returned to power. However, Aristide had to promise international financial institutions, such as the World Bank and the International Monetary Fund, that he would remove public subsidies for essential items, such as fuel. The combination of fuel shortages and subsequent increases in fuel prices left Haiti's poor without a way to cook their food.

A charcoal vendor works on a street in the commune of Pétionville in Port-au-Prince. Wood charcoal is the main source of home fuel in Haiti.

As a result, Haitians increased their use of charcoal, which is produced by the partial burning of wood at high temperatures, as an alternative fuel source. This increased demand for charcoal meant that the rate of deforestation in Haiti rose steeply, as Haitians begun to cut down their last forests to produce charcoal.

INTERNATIONAL COOPERATION

While large global institutions have created the conditions for environmental disaster, small, grassroots organizations from abroad may hold the key to salvation for Haiti's people and forests.

One example is the Brazilian Institute for Permaculture and Eco-villages (IPEC), which hosted members of Haiti's Papaye Peasant Movement at its headquarters near Brasilia. The two groups discussed techniques that IPEC is developing to allow small farmers to modify their practices so that their farms are environmentally sustainable over the long term.

Haiti has four national parks: Forêt des Pins, near the Dominican border; Parc La Visite, southwest of Port-au-Prince; Parc Macaya in southwestern Haiti; and Parc Historique La Citadelle in Cap-Haïtien. Although these parks were established to protect Haiti's native wildlife and plants, there are no government funds to protect these areas from incursions. As a result, some of these parks have already been partially deforested.

In 2012, the problem of protecting the environment versus the needs of a desperate people came to a head. President Michel Martelly, determined to enforce a new environmental protection effort, ordered people residing in Parc La Visite to leave. Police were sent in to evict the illegal squatters. The people resisted, explaining they had nowhere to go. As things tend to go in Haiti, the initiative ended up with police firing tear gas, then shooting and killing four people. They also destroyed the houses of the residents.

When the park was established in the 1980s, people living on the land were ordered to leave. The park boundaries had never been clearly established, and some of the people held titles to the land that went back decades. The evacuation order was never enforced and, naturally, the

A woman grows corn, leeks, and carrots in La Visite National Park.

people ignored it. Now, suddenly, the government tried to assert its authority and the result was disaster. This is just one small example—there are countless others—that demonstrates how difficult the environmental situation in Haiti is today.

It is IPEC's aim to create a similar learning center in the Western Caribbean to spread information about appropriate technologies for water and forest conservation. Some of the technologies they are teaching Haitians include building durable houses from adobe, a kind of dried mud, and using dry toilets that turn human waste into compost that enriches the soil.

There are scores of other non-profit organizations from many countries trying to do some good in Haiti. In many ways, small groups can sometimes find success that large-scale efforts cannot. For example, Project Gaia, a US nongovernmental non-profit group, is working to swap out Haitian peasant's wood-burning cook stoves for clean ethanol-fueled cook stoves. The group believes the country's infrastructure is already in place to produce ethanol. This would not only address the charcoal and deforestation problem, but help with air pollution and health problems as well.

Hundreds of farmers demand more space to grow their crops in the city of Hinche.

A woman cooks on a charcoal stove at a makeshift camp in Port-au-Prince shortly after the 2010 earthquake.

POVERTY AND THE ENVIRONMENT

In Haiti, protecting the environment really means protecting the poor. Haitians do not want to destroy their forests, but they also do not want to starve to death or watch their children waste away from malnutrition. Whether they cut wood for charcoal, for fuel, or to make handicrafts, they are just trying to survive in whatever way they can.

As long as Haitians continue to rank among the poorest in the world, environmental issues will take a second place to survival. Average Haitians struggle daily to survive and do not have the luxury to worry about issues about the environment. Unfortunately, environmental destruction affects those living closest to the land first—and that means the poor farmers.

In the past, international organizations have been both a help and hindrance, but they may be the best hope for Haiti's future. Haitians themselves are organizing for sustainable change, and with a little help from their overseas friends, they just might manage to turn round an environmental

disaster that has indirectly contributed to their chronic poverty. It's hard to interest desperate people in long-term solutions, when they need a short-term solution to where their next meal is coming from. Ironically, or cruelly, long-term plans are the only solutions that will really make a difference.

A worker cares for saplings in a tree nursery run by the environmental group Fondation Seguin in La Visite National Park.

INTERNET LINKS

www.grassrootsonline.org/term/peasant-movement-papaye-mpp
A number of good articles, with photos, about Haiti's environmental challenges can be found here.

phys.org/news/2015-06-northern-haiti-efforts-focus-coastlines.html
This article details conservation efforts along Haiti's northern coasts.

projectgaia.com/projects/haiti
The Project Gaia stove initiative is explained here.

HAITIANS

Teens play soccer in Cité Soleil, a desperately poor section of the Port-au-Prince metropolitan area.

THE TAÍNO ARAWAK, HAITI'S original inhabitants, were peace-loving farmers and hunters who were all but annihilated through forced labor and diseases brought by the Spanish. Few traces remain of the indigenous people. The current population of 10.1 million almost entirely consists of the descendants of some five hundred thousand or more Africans, who were brought to Haiti as slaves to work on the plantations.

Some internationally well-known Haitians include rapper Wyclef Jean (b. 1969), actress Garcelle Beauvais (b. 1966), writer Edwidge Danticat (b. 1969), and artist John James Audubon (1785-1851).

A Haitian family sits at the entrance to their home.

One year after the quake, great swaths of Port-au-Prince were still a shambles.

Whites and mulattoes—Haitians of mixed African and European descent— are minorities. Together they make up less than 5 percent of the population, but they hold most of the country's power and wealth.

POPULATION PRESSURES

Haiti has about 988 people per square mile (380 per square km), one of the highest population densities in the world. Although the population growth rate has halved since the 1950s, dropping to less than 2 percent from 4 percent per year, the lack of arable land and reliance on subsistence farming as a means of making a living have continued to put Haiti under enormous pressure. Only about 42 percent of Haitians live in rural areas, but they are concentrated in the most agriculturally productive mountain slopes and in the valleys.

Port-au-Prince, with more than two million inhabitants, is by far the largest city. Other major cities include Cap Haïtien and Gonaïves. Migration to the urban centers tends to be low, as urban unemployment is high and city life is just as harsh as in rural areas. Most Haitians prefer to try and eke out a living on their tiny plot of land in the countryside. Due to the high level of land ownership, migration between rural areas is almost negligible. Most of the people who do move to the city, especially to Port-au-Prince, are women who take jobs in the manufacturing or service sectors.

MULATTOES

Descendants of European colonists and African slaves, mulattoes control the government and most of the professions—in other words, the destiny of the country. Mulattoes have less influence in business and commerce, as trading was traditionally seen as a mercantile occupation that was beneath the educated middle and upper classes. However, this attitude is changing as mulattoes realize how much there is to be gained financially from business enterprises.

To the mulatto, skin color is very important. Those with a lighter skin tone are considered by fellow Haitians to be more intelligent and generally superior. In the eighteenth century, Haitians developed elaborate tables of genetic descent, dividing mulattoes into over a hundred shades of black and white. These ranged from the *Sacatra* (sah-kah-TRAH), which is seven-eighths black, to the several varieties of *Sangmêlés* (sahn-may-LAY), which are only one-sixteenth black. Strictly speaking, the term "mulatto" used to mean someone who is half black and half white. In the United States, the word is largely considered outdated and even offensive, in favor of "mixed" or "multiethnic" or simply African American or black. However, throughout Latin America, the term still carries a great deal of significance.

Today mulattoes are still very conscious of class divisions, and even within such a small group, there are differentiations based on skin color, wealth, and behavior. Mulattoes therefore strive to be as French, as white, and as Westernized in their lifestyle as possible.

Despite a common heritage with blacks, Haitian mulattoes do not feel any sense of racial kinship with them. Far from helping blacks improve their lot, mulattoes typically treat them with disdain and contempt, which reinforces the mulattoes' sense of superiority.

A group of captured Africans are led away by a white slaver in this illustration from 1868.

The ancestors of most of today's Haitians were Africans, who were brought to the New World as part of the notorious Triangle Trade. In the trade, ships from Europe traded money and trinkets for slaves in Africa, unloaded the slaves in the Caribbean, and then returned to Europe with sugar and other commodities. Some Africans were seized by slave-hunters during night raids, while others were taken as prisoners of war during tribal wars and later sold to the European slave traders.

Most slaves came from the Coromantee, Eboe, Mandingo, and Yoruba peoples. Chained to each other, they were thrown into the ship's hold, where the ceiling was so low they could not even sit up. At sailing time, members of the crew stood by with lighted torches and threatened to set fire to the ship if anyone attempted to escape. Once their homeland was no longer in sight, the slaves were allowed to come up on deck for a few minutes of exercise, always chained in pairs. Conditions were so atrocious that more than one in ten died during the trip, which took between six and twelve weeks. Some were struck down by disease, others committed suicide.

A few days before arrival in the New World, the people were fed well to fatten them up, and their bodies were rubbed with oil to make them look healthy. Once off the ship, they were paraded through the streets of Port-au-Prince before being taken to the market for auction.

BLACK HAITIANS

When they were slaves, Haiti's mostly black population had no rights and were treated like animals—or worse. After independence, they were still poor and were tied to a harsh land that yielded little food for their families. The lot of today's black Haitians has not changed much. Although free to move about, they are still slaves to the land and to their poverty.

Black Haitians' distrust and dislike of whites and mulattoes are deep-rooted. Having been oppressed for so long, first by the European colonizers, then by the Americans, and finally by the Haitian mulatto elite, it is not surprising that most black Haitians are wary of any moves that could be interpreted as attempts to subjugate them.

Although Catholicism and the French language officially predominated throughout most of Haiti's history, it is the vodou religion and the Creole language—both unique Haitian adaptations of their African and European roots—that pervade the life of the black Haitian.

Haitian children smile in a refugee camp in the Dominican Republic.

HAITIAN DRESS

Typical of the Caribbean, Haitian clothing is extremely colorful and made of lightweight cotton to suit the tropical climate. In the urban centers, men wear short-sleeved shirts and cotton trousers; women usually wear full skirts and simple wide-necked blouses in bright colors and patterns.

Clothing takes up a large portion of poor families' income. Women typically sew their family's clothes themselves from the cheapest available materials. When Alaska became part of the United States, an enterprising

Throughout Haiti's tumultuous past, hundreds of thousands of Haitians have fled their homes to seek refuge in countries that offer greater political stability and a better standard of living.

The first wave of emigration out of Haiti came during the US occupation, when poor and dispossessed farmers were "invited" to work in Cuba and the Dominican Republic. The Americans at that time owned large sugarcane plantations in these two countries and were short of labor. Since then, most migrants to the Dominican Republic have more or less assimilated into the local society.

In the second wave were professionals and educated Haitians fleeing the repressive Duvalier regimes. Teachers, artists, politicians who opposed Papa Doc and Baby Doc's policies, and administrators of international organizations were granted asylum in such cities as Paris, New York, and Montreal. They were later joined by skilled workers and technicians.

The emigration of skilled workers and trained professionals has only made Haiti's economic and social problems worse. Given Haiti's bleak prospects, however, it is not surprising that these emigrants left, and it is unlikely that they will soon return to their native homeland.

The most recent wave of emigrants includes manual workers, taxi drivers, and laborers. Most of them are living abroad illegally, especially in the United States.

In all, it is estimated that a third of all Haitians are living outside their country. In the United States, about 197,000 Haitian immigrants live in the greater Miami area, while another 158,000 are living in the greater New York City area.

Emigration to France is a more recent phenomenon. Often illegal immigrants manage to get into France from Haiti via one of France's overseas territories, such as Martinique, Guadeloupe, or French Guiana.

American businessman started exporting obsolete forty-eight-star flags to Haiti at rock-bottom prices. Soon after, many Haitian families could be seen sporting the outdated American flag on their backs.

Rural Haitians have a set of clothes that they reserve for special occasions. Shoes are also equally treasured and kept with care. Some going to Port-au-Prince walk barefoot and carry their shoes to the edge of town before putting them on. At home or in the fields, people go bare-foot or wear homemade sandals fashioned out of whatever materials are at hand—even old automobile tires.

Vendors sell clothes on the streets of the Iron Market in the capital city.

INTERNET LINKS

www.migrationpolicy.org/article/haitian-immigrants-united-states
This site offers statistics and interactive maps.

www.washingtonpost.com/news/worldviews/wp/2015/06/16/the-bloody-origins-of-the-dominican-republics-ethnic-cleansing-of-haitians
This article examines the Dominican Republic's ethnic hatred of Haitians.

LIFESTYLE

A street vendor balances his merchandise on his head as he makes his way down a crowded street in downtown Port-au-Prince.

7

F OR MANY HAITIANS, EVERYDAY LIFE is defined by the struggle to recover from the 2010 earthquake. More than five years after the catastrophe, large numbers of people still live without electricity, clean water, or sanitation facilities. Makeshift camps for earthquake survivors, intended to be temporary, have become permanent living places. Nevertheless, life goes on. For most Haitians, it is a life of poverty, hard work, simplicity, community spirit, and—when possible—celebration.

These people live in humble, often one-room dwellings, believe in vodou, have very little education, join together in common-law marriages, and speak Creole. At the other end of the societal spectrum, upper-class Haitians live in grand houses, practice Catholicism, speak French, and are educated abroad.

The middle class is still a small segment of Haitian society. Composed of blacks *and* mulattoes, these Haitians are somewhat less concerned about color and family background. Most emphasize education and the use of French in order to progress professionally and improve their standard of living.

Curiously, perhaps, for such a poor nation, Haiti has the lowest crime rate in the Caribbean. However, its crime statistics are unreliable and are thought by many international organizations to be inaccurate or underreported.

SOCIAL DIVISIONS

UPPER CLASS The Haitian upper class makes up less than 5 percent of the population. It is composed mostly of mulattoes, but well-educated and wealthy blacks are also included. Upper-class Haitians are Roman Catholic, lead a Westernized lifestyle, and tend to show an appreciation of all things French. They generally emphasize elegance and refinement in everything they do. Socializing often takes place after church on Sundays and in private clubs.

The elite live in a closed, almost caste-like society. Membership in the group is almost always determined by birth. Elite people marry among themselves. The upper-class family is one where the parents are legally married and the mother stays at home to look after the children.

The elite live and work in the cities. Its members own much of the urban land, which they rent out to the people working in factories and offices. The men tend to favor the more gentlemanly professions of law, medicine, and architecture. Most women, although often well-educated, do not work outside the home.

A relatively well-off family prepares dinner.

The family has remained the focal point of love and loyalty. Since the group is so small and intermarriage is the norm, most people are related to one another.

MIDDLE CLASS The middle class is a relatively new phenomenon in Haiti, brought about by wider educational opportunities and industrialization. Since the Duvalier period, the size and political clout of the middle class has continued to grow. Middle-class families see education as a means of achieving higher status. They speak French and typically work as civil servants, shopkeepers, technicians, and teachers.

URBAN LOWER CLASS The urban lower class makes up about half the urban population. Most members of this class came to the cities in search of work and now live in the slums that proliferate on the edge of town. Unemployment is high, and many people work for themselves, eking out a living as lottery ticket sellers, artisans, or market women. Those who have jobs are mostly employed in the service sector as domestics, shoe shiners, or day laborers. The urban lower class works extremely hard to try and achieve a better standard of living. Their communities still display some aspects of rural living; people are always ready to help one another, and communal activities are common.

The famous Iron Market in Port-au-Prince, destroyed in the earthquake, and since restored, is a marketplace with some nine hundred vendors.

RURAL LOWER CLASS Poor farmers make up most of the Haitian population. They are at the bottom of the social ladder, and most live in abject poverty. They grow their own food and live in shacks made of a few sheets of corrugated iron nailed together. These shacks have few, if any, modern amenities. Authority is held by the eldest male member of the family, but it is usually the woman who runs the family's daily affairs.

A few farmers own larger land holdings and consequently have a better standard of living. They are called *groneg* (groh NEGG) or *grozabitan* (grohzah-bih-TAHN), and both expressions mean "a person of wealth and power." They are usually the leaders in their communities and become the local *chef de section* (shefdeh sec-SIOHN), serving as a link between the local and the national governments.

PUBLIC SAFETY

Today, two main law enforcement entities patrol Haiti. The Haitian National Police (PNH) functions as both a civilian police force and something of

TONTONS MACOUTE

In 1959 President François Duvalier ("Papa Doc") set up a private police force to consolidate his power and protect himself against the army, which he feared. First called the Milice Civile, the force's name was changed to Volontaires de la Sécurité Nationale, or "National Security Volunteers," better known as Tontons Macoute, or just Macoutes. Haitians used that name for the paramilitary force, in reference to the Haitian Creole mythological character Tonton Macoute (Uncle Gunnysack). He is a bogeyman who kidnaps and punishes unruly children by snaring them in a gunny sack, or macoute, and eating them.

Macoutes were characterized by their unwavering loyalty to the president and their use of extreme violence. Their tactics included torture, kidnapping, and murder, and their activities were above the law. At the height of their reign of terror, there were around ten thousand Macoutes spread all over the country. A hardcore group of two thousand was based in Port-au-Prince. Most were drawn from the urban black lower class and personally selected by Duvalier. Rural Macoutes wore a uniform of faded denim and carried old rifles, while urban macoutes dressed in shiny blue suits and carried pistols.

As only the trusted elite within the force were paid a salary, Macoutes had the right to extort money from the population and to accept bribes. At the daily roadblocks they operated in and around Port-au-Prince, they exacted a toll from all motorists. A Macoute also had the right to force his way into any house and demand to be fed.

After the fall of the Duvalier regime in 1986, Macoutes were hunted down by a population enraged by decades of terror, and many were lynched in the streets. The force was officially disbanded, but plainclothes squads of attachés (ah-tah-CHAY), paramilitary vigilantes modeled on the Macoutes, continued to operate under the control of Haiti's national chief of police. Following the October 1993 blockade of international police monitors and the murder of unknown numbers of Haitians, the United Nations Security Council called for the disarming of attachés. Aristide disbanded the police and replaced them with new recruits.

a de facto army. The actual army was disbanded in 1995. The PNH, which employees about nine thousand people, includes a unit in charge of presidential security. Like so much else in Haiti, the PNH is hampered by mismanagement, corruption, and underfunding.

The other policing unit in Haiti is temporary, but has been in the country since 2004. The United Nations Stabilization Mission in Haiti (MINUSTAH) is a peacekeeping force. Such units are typically sent into war-torn countries, which Haiti is not. However, after the coup and subsequent exile of Jean-Bertrand Aristide, the UN determined the situation in Haiti to be so fraught that it was a threat to international peace and security. MINUSTAH forces were originally led by the Brazilian army and later expanded to include other Latin American forces. The force, which is much disliked by Haitians, focuses much of its work on fighting political unrest and gang activities, and has been accused of human rights violations of its own.

Following the 2010 earthquake, the UN extended MINUSTAH's mission. Meanwhile, military personnel from many other countries, including the

A member of the **MINUSTAH** force fires tear gas at demonstrators during a protest against the government in December 2014.

United States, entered the country for the purposes of distributing food, water, other necessities, and medical aid. Some of these factions were also accused of grievous misconduct. The forces from Nepal, for example, were found to be guilty of certain atrocities, as well as being the inadvertent source of the cholera epidemic which swept the country after the quake. Nevertheless, the UN claims that, on the whole, MINUSTAH forces have helped to stabilize the country.

A Brazilian soldier of the MINUSTAH force gives food to a child orphaned by the earthquake.

EDUCATION

Although public education is free, textbooks and other school materials are not. As a result, many children, especially those in rural areas, cannot afford to go to school. The dropout rate for all levels is very high, especially in rural areas.

The best education is offered by private schools. These schools are mostly run by religious groups, such as the Roman Catholic Church and certain Protestant denominations. Some religious organizations offer a complete range of education from kindergarten through to high school.

ELEMENTARY Kindergartens are operated by elementary schools and are the most attended of all schools. Children go to kindergarten for two years, generally at the age of three or four, and then move on to elementary school for another six years. Instruction is in Creole until the last few years, when children start learning French to prepare them for high school education. Primary school enrollment increased recently to 80 percent, but few children complete the full course.

HIGH SCHOOL Not many children manage to attend secondary school, especially in rural areas where they are often needed to work the family farm. There are also few high schools in the countryside—children may have to walk several miles to get to the nearest school—and classes are typically large. Rural children who graduate from elementary school often have to move to town to continue their education. Some vocational schools have boarding facilities, and the government gives out scholarships to defray the cost of lodging. High school lasts seven years with a very demanding national examination at the end; many students drop out in the last two years. Instruction is in French and rote learning is the norm. About a quarter of the high school population attends vocational schools.

POST-SECONDARY The largest university is the State University of Haiti. Founded in 1944, its faculties include Law and Economics, Administration and Management, and Medicine and Pharmacy. There are two private universities, the University of Roi Henri Christophe and the International Institute of University Studies. Haiti also has a number of law schools and technical colleges.

Students do homework at a local school in Cité Soleil, one of the poorest sections of Port-au-Prince.

HEALTH AND WELFARE

Women wash clothes in a stream.

Healthcare is a problem in Haiti as most homes do not have running water and people have to use a river for personal and household washing. Regular contact with polluted rivers and streams puts Haitians at risk of developing chronic diseases carried by waterborne germs and parasitic worms. Malaria is also prevalent. Most Haitians suffer from nutritional deficiencies bordering on malnutrition. Average life expectancy is only sixty-three years. This lack of clean water and sanitary facilities helped to spread the cholera outbreak in 2010, ten months after the country was devastated by the earthquake.

Medical facilities are poor, and most are located in the urban areas. Most rural dwellers consult a vodou priest when they need medical help, which only aggravates matters in some cases. There are not enough hospitals or beds, even if more people could reach a hospital when seriously ill. Supplementing the public health system, there are a number of clinics, mostly in villages and shantytowns, usually run by religious groups. Public hospitals and outpatient treatment are free, but patients must bring their own food and buy their own medical supplies.

HOUSING

Housing for most Haitians is extremely basic. Few Haitians have running water, and 40 percent lack access to clean drinking water. Only one in five have access to a sanitary toilet. Poor urban Haitians who are employed usually rent one or two rooms as living accommodation for their whole family, while those who have no job or income are forced to live in squatter shacks that are roughly nailed together from whatever scrap materials can be picked up from the local garbage dumps. These squatter shacks have no running water or electricity. Hundreds of thousands of Haitians live in shantytowns, some of which are so overcrowded that shacks are literally built one on top of another.

MALNUTRITION

Most Haitians eat only one small meal a day and their calorie intake is the lowest in the Americas. According to some estimates, approximately 20 percent of children in Haiti below the age of five are malnourished. Lack of food and inadequate nutrition have led to the widespread occurrence of chronic and often fatal diseases. Kwashiorkor, a disease caused by the lack of protein, which may  *lead to permanent mental and physical disability, is widespread among children. Poor rural Haitian children are at least 6 inches (15 cm) shorter and 50 pounds (23 kg) lighter than American children of the same age, and most grow up into weak adults with little resistance to disease.*

Houses in rural areas are built of wattle covered with a layer of mud or plaster that is whitewashed. Floors are made of pounded earth, and the roof is usually covered with straw or sheet iron. Very basic kitchen facilities are located outside the house. Furnishings, in rural areas as well as in urban working-class areas, are sparse and simple. In large families, children sleep on mats on the floor.

Upper-class Haitians, on the other hand, live in ornate mansions with gingerbread wood embellishments and ironwork filigree, or in large new houses built of stone or concrete in the European style with all the modern amenities.

Between 60 to 80 percent of the Haitian population lives in poverty. Most are poor farmers who try to scratch a living out of an uncooperative land. Their lifestyle has remained virtually unchanged throughout the history of the country. Because most farmers own their own land, they find it difficult to break away from their traditional way of life, thus perpetuating their dependence on the land and their poverty.

Plots are typically too small to enable farmers to grow sufficient food for their families. Widespread soil erosion and a lack of irrigation have reduced the productivity of the soil, making it even harder for farmers to grow what they need. As families grow larger and land plots get divided, some people are left landless and have to resort to sharecropping—working for another farmer in return for some crops.

The plight of Haitian farmers was made worse when Haiti's economy was opened up to free trade after 1994. Farmers found that their products could not compete with cheaper imports, and their already meager incomes decreased further.

WOMEN

At the lower end of the social stratum, women play a vital economic role, shouldering much of the responsibility of providing food, income, clothing, and comfort for the family. Although men clear and prepare the fields for planting the family's food supply, women are responsible for growing the crops, transporting them, and selling them at the market. Women usually also have the responsibility of raising poultry and cattle, which they again take to the market. Lower-class rural women thus control almost every aspect of their families' domestic affairs.

Upper-class women are typically well educated—often abroad—but they usually do not have to work for a living. This is gradually changing, however, as increasingly difficult economic conditions and the desire for economic independence have led more and more upper- and middle-class women to join the work force, usually as teachers, nurses, bilingual secretaries, and other professionals.

Although Haitian women were granted the right to vote in 1950, few women have succeeded in politics. Ertha Pascal-Trouillot, the first and only female Haitian head of state, headed the interim government for a short while after the fall of Jean-Claude Duvalier. Four women were appointed to cabinet posts under the interim government.

INTERNET LINKS

aarondanowski.com/2015/06/13/week-2-everyday-life-in-port-au-prince
This blog entry by a young American visitor to Haiti gives an outsider's view at a typical day in Port-au-Prince.

www.cnn.com/2015/08/17/opinions/omalley-haiti-cholera-un
This article asserts the UN should take responsibility for Haiti's cholera epidemic.

www.foreignaffairs.com/articles/haiti/2015-06-21/house-hunters
This blistering article looks at "How Reconstruction in Haiti Went So Wrong."

www.hrw.org/world-report/2015/country-chapters/haiti
Human Rights Watch reviews Haiti's problems.

www.miamiherald.com/news/nation-world/world/americas/haiti/article6031617.html
The article "Rebuilding Haiti: Still a work in progress" looks at recovery efforts.

www.usatoday.com/videos/news/world/2015/01/09/21385117
Included is a video about life in Haiti that shows the sorts of homes that many people live in.

water.org/country/haiti
This organization reports on Haiti's water and sanitation situation.

RELIGION

A man prays in a new church built next to the
National Cathedral, which was destroyed in 2010.

8

A N OLD HAITIAN FOLK SAYING asserts that "Haiti is 90 percent Catholic and 100 percent vodou." That statement slyly sums up the country's religious situation better than any official statistics ever could.

The Spanish brought Roman Catholicism to Haiti. It was the only official religion in Haiti for centuries afterward. Nevertheless, black Haitians have kept alive the religious beliefs and practices of their African ancestors. Vodou (also spelled voodoo) was finally recognized as an

Mental health care is almost nonexistent in Haiti, where mental illness is greatly misunderstood and taboo. Catholic and Protestant church leaders and vodou practitioners often work to try to fill the void.

An acolyte participates in a Mass in St. Pierre Church in Pétionville.

official religion in 2003. Upper- and middle-class Haitians are, however, more likely to attend formal churches and observe Roman Catholic rituals.

Additional religions have slowly made their presence felt in Haiti: Mormons, Baptists, Methodists, Jehovah's Witnesses, and Seventh Day Adventists all have missions in Haiti. Some American missionaries intent on converting Haitians away from vodou—a religion they openly equate with the devil—have increased their activities at the grassroots level.

ROMAN CATHOLICISM

Roman Catholicism did not gain as strong a foothold in Haiti as in the Latin American countries. As early as 1805, the Haitian constitution provided for the separation of church and state, and it declared marriage to be a civil rather than a religious contract. For forty-five years after Haiti's independence, no priest set foot in the country. Nevertheless, Roman Catholicism remained the only official religion in Haiti until vodou was recognized almost two hundred years later.

Although most Haitians are Catholic, only mulattoes adhere strictly to Catholicism. To them, the Catholic religion is part and parcel of the French culture to which they aspire. The Church has become a symbol of their link with the outside world and a defense against the vodou religion of the black masses. The upper classes look upon vodou as a kind of black magic practiced by ignorant people.

Church services are also something of a ritual for the upper echelons of Haitian society, who see Sunday Mass as one of the main opportunities for socializing among themselves. Men dress in suits, and women wear elegant dresses and hats to go to church every Sunday morning. After Mass, the men gather to talk about business and politics, while the women exchange family news in the churchyard.

As Catholicism has traditionally been closely associated with the mulatto elite, black nationalists have always opposed the Church. François Duvalier had a running battle with the Roman Catholic clergy during much of his term in office. Duvalier eventually expelled from Haiti several provincial

Catholics pray during a service.

A woman takes part in a Day of the Dead celebrations at the Cemetery of Cité Soleil.

bishops and the bishop of Port-au-Prince, who was considered by Catholics to be the country's religious leader. Duvalier, in turn, was excommunicated by the Vatican.

Since then, the Catholic Church has done much to bridge the gap with the common people in Haiti. Priests now take more of an interest in the black Haitian community and have adopted a more pragmatic attitude to vodou. The election of Jean-Bertrand Aristide twice to the presidency increased the importance of the Church, since he had been a Catholic priest before entering politics.

VODOU

Vodou is the national religion of the Haitian people and a vital force in politics and culture. Derived from African ancestor worship, vodou has fused various African beliefs and rites with Catholicism to become a uniquely Haitian religion. Unlike other religions, it has no centralized church, no scriptures, and no theology. It is a participatory religion strongly rooted to Haiti and its particular cultural history. Vodou is a blend of beliefs that is celebrated through song, dance, and prayer.

The concept of sin does not exist in vodou. A person who acts in the wrong way does not offend the gods, but rather it is fellow human beings who suffer the consequences. Social and moral behavior is regulated by a set of taboos linked to ancestral values and traditions.

VODOU COSMOLOGY Vodou faith is centered on *loas* (LWAH), or spirits that communicate directly with humans in a state of trance. This is a psychological state induced by rhythmic dancing and music. Through possession, the distinctions between divine and mortal beings are blurred; one can become the other. The human body is animated by both a *gro-bon-ange* (groh-bohn-NAHNGE), "big guardian angel" and a *ti-bon-ange* (chih-bohn-NAHNGE), or "little guardian angel."

A man is possessed by the spirit Gede, the loa of Death.

These represent the soul and the cosmic consciousness. Upon death, the gro-bon-ange goes through several stages to become a loa.

The loas of African origin are called Rada, and those of Haitian origin are Petro. The three most important loas are Legba, Erzulie, and Danbala. Legba is the loa that links humans to the spirit world. He is invoked before any vodou ceremony is held. Erzulie is a female loa that closely resembles the Virgin Mary of the Catholic Church. Danbala is a loa in charge of rainfall. His symbol is a serpent, which, unlike the Christian symbol, is not evil.

A man passes a sacrificed chicken over a woman in a trance during a vodou ritual.

VODOU HIERARCHY The leaders of vodou religion are priests and priestesses called *houngan* (hoon-GAHN) and *mambo* respectively. Both sexes are equal, although the more demanding ceremonies are usually carried out by male priests. Vodou priests and priestesses have other jobs outside the priesthood and perform vodou ceremonies as a service to the people. During vodou ceremonies they are attended to by a group of helpers called *hounsis* (hoon-SEE).

VODOU RITUALS Vodou ceremonies are held to ask the blessing of a particular loa, to raise the spirit of the dead, or to place a curse on someone. The service usually takes place in a small enclosure with a thatched roof, often in the garden of the houngan or mambo. The temple is divided into two, with the inner chamber reserved for the priests and the initiated. The participants usually remain in the antechamber, where most of the ceremony is conducted. Patterns called *vevers* (veh-VAIR) are drawn on the floor in cornmeal to ward off evil spirits. The walls are hung with pictures of Catholic saints, flags, and stylized designs. A small altar holds sacred objects such as ceremonial clothes, vases, and vessels containing baked earth, rattles, and bells.

The Catholic influence is strong in the opening ceremony with the vodou priest blessing those present and everyone kneeling and making the sign of the cross. The loa is invoked by the priest to the sound of beating drums and rattles. Meanwhile the participants sing and dance in trance-like movements. The loa usually makes its wishes known through the houngan or an animal being sacrificed. Possession by a loa is a desirable conclusion to the ceremony because it is interpreted to mean that the loa has spoken through the chosen person's mouth, revealing divine will.

FOLK MEDICAL BELIEFS

A vodou priest holds a protective amulet.

When Haitians do not feel well, they usually do not go to a hospital or a clinic. Sickness and death are attributed to supernatural causes, so Haitians believe that only a vodou priest can cure them. As a form of preventive medicine, people wear amulets given to them by their priest.

The Haitian people have perfected the science of using plants and herbs to cure sickness, and the use of herbal medicines is widespread. Chamomile is used to reduce swellings and tumors, hogwood bark to promote urination, soursop as a sedative, the wild plum leaf to reduce chills, and cedar bark to treat diarrhea.

Some medical beliefs are less benign and can be health-endangering. Vodou priests sometimes advise that cow's milk is "too strong" for infants, that goat's milk is bad for infants, and that meat of all kinds is not good for the young. All these beliefs only serve to worsen the problem of malnutrition among Haitian children.

ZOMBIES

The Haitian belief in zombies is rooted in the traditions brought by enslaved Africans. It was thought that the vodou deity Baron Samedi would gather them from graves and bring them to a heaven-like afterlife in Africa. That is, unless the person had offended the deity in some way, in which case he or she would be a slave forever after death.

Two types of zombies exist in the tradition, one being an enslaved body, a body without a soul. It is physically revived by a bokor sorcerer, a witch-like figure, and used for its strength and lack of will. The other is an incorporeal zombie—the "zombie astral"—the enslaved soul held in a bottle and sold for advantages in luck, healing, or business achievement. This type, it is understood, is a temporary entity, as God will eventually take back the soul.

Haitians are not afraid of zombies, but would rather not encounter them. Their greatest fear is to become one themselves. In the soulless zombie, the Haitian sees everything that is despicable: loss of the powers of perception and loss of self-control. For a Haitian, no fate is more terrible. To prevent their deceased from being turned into zombies, Haitians take several precautions before burying their dead. These include stabbing the corpse in the heart with a knife before burial, and clipping the hair and nails of the deceased and burying the clippings with the body.

PROTESTANT MISSIONARIES

Since the mid-1800s, a variety of Protestant denominations have sent missions to Haiti to convert Haitians from vodou and Roman Catholicism. Today about 29 percent of Haitians are Protestant. The largest Protestant groups are the Baptists, who make up 15 percent, and the Pentecostals, who make up 8 percent of all Protestants in Haiti. Other Protestant groups include Methodists, Episcopalians, and Jehovah's Witnesses.

When François Duvalier wanted to establish a counterforce to the conservative and pro-upper-class Roman Catholic Church, he facilitated the work of American Pentecostal missionaries in Haiti.

Christian missionaries continue their opposition to vodou and some related aspects of Haiti's indigenous culture even today. Lately there has been an enormous influx of Protestant denominations, mostly from the United

States. With their large financial resources, they attract a lot of hungry and destitute people, putting them to work at their missions in return for food.

Missions have traditionally been very active in education in rural and urban areas. Historically, religious organizations, including the Catholic Church, often provided the only schools for rural people. Today some Protestant churches continue to run such schools as the Episcopalian St. Vincent's Center for Handicapped Children, part of the Children's Medical Mission of Haiti.

INTERNET LINKS

www.huffingtonpost.com/2015/01/14/voodoo-haiti-mental-health_n_6471624.html
This Reuters article reports how vodou priests and doctors address mental health issues in a traumatized nation.

www.miamiherald.com/news/nation-world/world/americas/haiti/article16946363.html
This is a report about recent violence against Catholic nuns in Haiti.

news.nationalgeographic.com/news/2002/10/1021_021021_taboovoodoo.html
This article explains some common misconceptions of vodou.

www.nytimes.com/2012/10/31/opinion/a-zombie-is-a-slave-forever.html
This intriguing article posits a spiritual and cultural connection between slavery and the concept of the zombie.

www.usccb.org/issues-and-action/human-life-and-dignity/haiti/haiti-reconstruction-project.cfm
The US Conference of Catholic Bishops reports on church progress in the reconstruction of Haiti.

LANGUAGE

A volunteer reads a French picture book to an orphaned child waiting to be adopted after the earthquake.

9

F OR MORE THAN A CENTURY AFTER its independence, French was the only official language of Haiti, even though most of its population could not understand it. French is the language of refinement and a passport to social promotion. The use of language in Haiti highlights the polarities in its society.

On the other hand, virtually every Haitian understands and speaks Creole. It is the language of everyday life. It was only in 1987, when the new constitution was adopted, that Creole was granted legal status.

Two little brothers share a desk in the front of the class and listen to their teacher, only a few weeks after the earthquake.

Haitian Creole is a lively and colorful language. It expresses the very soul of the Haitian people, their wisdom and sense of humor. Creole conversation is sprinkled with proverbs that tell of fatalism and resignation, and of the cunning and carefulness needed when faced with the powerful in Haitian society. Here are a few examples:

- *On an unlucky day, sour cream might break your skull and a sweet potato peel might cut your foot.*
- *Do not insult the crocodile's mother before crossing the river.*
- *The donkey does the work, while the horse gets the medal.*

FRENCH

Even though French was the only official language of Haiti until 1987, a tiny percentage of the population speaks it. At the elementary school level, the medium of instruction is Creole in the first few years, and children learn French almost as a foreign language. In high school, classes are conducted solely in French. As less than 20 percent of Haitian children complete elementary school, it is not surprising that their knowledge of French is so limited.

Given its exclusivity, French is considered by Haitians to be a sign of superiority. Its use is restricted almost exclusively to the urban upper and middle classes. French is always used on formal public occasions and sometimes at formal private functions as well. Upper-class Haitians speak French whenever they meet—in church, at the club, and at other social events. At home they are likely to speak both French and Creole, sometimes using words from both languages in the same sentence.

For the urban middle class, the use of French is essential in moving up the social ladder. Middle-class Haitians always insist on speaking French, even in informal settings, to prove that they are worthy of belonging to the upper class, and they make sure their children do not speak Creole—something they see as a bad habit of the lower classes.

Haitians are a warm and hospitable people. A huge billboard proclaiming "Welcome to Haiti" in French greets visitors to the island, and it is typical for Haitians to smile and call out "Bonjour, blanc!" (bohn-djoor BLAHN), or "Hi there, white!" whenever they see a Caucasian visitor on the street. Haitians are careful to show respect to one another, despite their

characteristic lack of formality. When visiting friends, they say "honneur" (on-NERH), or "honor", when they arrive; the host replies with "respect" (reh-SPAY), or "respect."

CREOLE

Haitian Creole was originally a *lingua franca*, or pidgin, used as a means of communication among the Haitian slaves, who spoke a number of different African languages, and between slaves and their French-speaking masters. Now a full-fledged language with its own grammar and spelling system and the sole language of most Haitians, Creole is finally recognized as one of Haiti's official languages.

STANDARDIZATION OF CREOLE At first Creole was only a spoken language. Its vocabulary consisted of French and African words pronounced in a distinctive Haitian way, but there was no standard spelling system. Although some writers wrote in Creole in the early 1920s, they spelled words arbitrarily, according to their own conventions.

Students and teachers rally in Cap-Haitien, asking for improvements to the education system. The signs are written in Creole.

It was not until the early 1940s that an attempt was made at devising a standardized spelling. Two Americans, Ormonde McConnell and Frank Laubach, established a phonetic alphabet in which each sound was represented by a single symbol. This system was later modified by Haitian linguists Charles-Fernand Pressoir and Lelio Faubles using certain conventions of the French alphabet. Present-day Creole grammatical structures and spelling developed from these early works.

CHARACTERISTICS OF CREOLE Haitian Creole is a dynamic language, reflecting foreign influences and characterized by the invention of new words and structures. Although most words are of French origin, African and Spanish words have also left their mark, and Creole grammar and syntax are influenced by African grammatical structures. Haitian Creole is also a linguistically economic language. Thoughts and actions are expressed using a minimum of words, determinants and prepositions are used sparingly,

> ## CREOLES AROUND THE WORLD
>
> *Creole languages spring up when groups of people who speak different languages make contact with each other and need to develop a quick way of communicating without learning each other's native language. As Europeans explored other continents, set up trading relations with other peoples, and transported slaves from Africa to the New World, a number of Creole languages based on European languages developed around the world.*
>
> *From English came Gullah, spoken off the coast of South Carolina; Sranantongo, spoken in Suriname; and Pidgin English, which still flourishes in Melanesia (New Hebrides, the Solomon Islands, and New Guinea), Hawaii, and Papua New Guinea. From French there are the Creoles of Haiti, Louisiana, and the Lesser Antilles, and from Pidgin Spanish and Portuguese there is the Papiamento of Curaçao. Easier to learn than the native languages of so many different countries, Creole languages are often indispensable as a means of communication, as an educational tool, and in politics.*

and words are simplified. When certain long words are shortened, they become the same as other short words, so intonation is important in helping to distinguish between words.

NEWSPAPERS

The first newspaper in Haiti was published in 1764. *Affiches Américaines* reported on commercial, cultural, and agricultural events. Today, there are two daily French newspapers and a number of weekly publications in French and Creole. The two daily newspapers *Le Nouvelliste* and *Le Matin* were founded in 1898 and 1908, respectively. Newspapers in Haiti tend to focus on local gossip, cultural events, and sports, and are mostly quite thin, ranging from four to eight pages. Due to widespread poverty and illiteracy, most Haitians do not rely on the print media for news.

A Haitian French language newspaper shows Haiti's ousted President Jean-Bertrand Aristide.

Historically, freedoms of the press and of expression in Haiti, though constitutionally protected, were free in name only. The press has long endured a rigorous system of censorship and repression. During the Duvalier regimes, newspapers were not allowed to publish anything that could be construed as criticism of the government. Throughout Haitian history, journalists have been persecuted, imprisoned, shot, and exiled for falling afoul of the ruling party.

However, over the last decade, the situation has improved significantly, with a marked downturn in violence against journalists. Still, the situation is far from ideal. An article of the constitution says that the government must publicize all laws, international agreements, treaties, and contracts, though the government generally makes it difficult for journalists to access that information.

The teledyòl, (tay-lay-DIOHL), or "grapevine," is the most common, though not the most reliable, way of spreading news in Haiti. Foreign news is limited, with only AFP (Agence France Presse) providing an international service. Not much space is given to crime news, and political news is confined to official releases.

RADIO AND TELEVISION

Since the national daily newspapers are limited to the Port-au-Prince area and few Haitians can read, radio is more important than print in disseminating news throughout the country. There are many radio stations, most of them privately owned and operating regionally. Broadcasts are in French and Creole. However, the vast majority of the population still does not own a radio and thus has no access to public information.

There are several television stations broadcasting in Haiti. The national television station is the government-owned *Television Nationale d'Haiti*, which broadcasts programs in Creole, French, and Spanish. The other stations are privately-owned.

ILLITERACY

Haiti has traditionally had a poor record on literacy. Before independence, there were no schools in Haiti and the colonialists simply sent their children to France to be educated. After independence, the state continued to neglect education, providing only a minimal elementary and high school system, doing little to address the poverty that still forces so many Haitian children to abandon school at an early age and failing to offer elementary and secondary education in their native Creole language.

In 1985, according to UNESCO estimates, the average rate of adult illiteracy was 62.4 percent, the highest in the Western hemisphere, with a staggering 85 percent rate in rural areas. After the introduction of basic adult education programs in Creole, illiteracy has fallen to 40 percent in 2015, according to the CIA.

INTERNET LINKS

freedomhouse.org/report/freedom-press/2014/haiti#.VeT3F7cb6Lg
The state of freedom of the press in Haiti is evaluated here.

haitihub.wordpress.com
Haitihub's mission is to help people speak Creole, connect, and do more.

www.kreyol.com/creole-phrases
This site offers useful words and phrases in Haitian Creole.

www.omniglot.com/writing/haitiancreole.htm
Omniglot gives an introduction to Haitian Creole.

Haitian-born American rap star Wyclef Jean ran for president in the same election that Michel Martelly eventually won. Wyclef also organized some charities to help his homeland.

10

HAITIANS ADORN THEIR WORLD WITH brilliant color. They have married the culture of their African ancestors with French influence to produce a unique Haitian style. The canvas does not matter: pictures, buses, churches, houses, public buildings, or simply lamp posts—they are painted brightly, without restraint.

A Haitian artist exhibits his creations at the Grand Market during the Caribbean Festival of Arts in 2015.

Before he became Haiti's president in 2011, Michel Martelly was one of the country's best-known musicians. He was a singer and keyboardist who went by the stage name "Sweet Micky." His music, called compas, is a modern merengue musical genre with European and African roots.

A taptap bus driver maneuvers his vehicle in the heavy traffic of Port-au-Prince.

Even the Casernes Dessalines—the notorious military barracks where so many Haitians have been tortured—is drenched in pure yellow, contrasting magnificently with the intense blue sky. From the intercity taptaps, or public buses that display a collage of flamboyant decorations, homespun proverbs, and religious quotations, to the vodou dancing that is performed both as a religious celebration and to welcome tourists to the elegant old villas of Port-au-Prince, Haiti displays a deep and varied artistic spirit.

MUSIC AND DANCE

The Haitian soul comes alive in dancing. In Haiti, dancing to the beat of the drum is a means of communication as well as a celebration of life. Everyone dances in Haiti, including the very young and the very old. They dance to celebrate a festival, to express their gratitude for a bountiful harvest, or to forget their poverty.

Haitian music and dancing have changed very little since the days of slavery on the sugar plantations. Most dances were born of vodou, and a vodou ceremony always concludes with a dance. Today there is ritual dancing as well as dancing *pouplaisi* (poo play-ZEE), or "for pleasure." One of the most popular dance styles in Haiti is the *merengue* (muh-REN-gay). An eye-catching dance with sinuous and languorous movements, it is enjoyed by the elite and the urban lower classes alike. The songs that accompany the merengue are often full of innuendo concerning love or politics.

A Rara band performs while walking down a street.

Haitian music, like other Caribbean varieties, is based on four beats. However, local musicians bring in variations that alter the rhythm. In the merengue, for example, a weak beat always follows the strong salvo of drums.

LITERATURE

In the nineteenth century, many educated and wealthy Haitians devoted themselves to the study of fine arts in the classical French tradition. At the beginning of the twentieth century, however, the literary focus shifted to native Haitian folklore and literary values.

Haitian writers often used poems and essays to express their nationalistic fervor and deep anguish at foreign domination. Jean Price-Mars was an innovator in Haitian literature who supported the concept of *négritude* (nay-grih-TUHD)—pride in being black and in the African heritage. His novel *Ainsi Parla l'Oncle* (*Thus Spoke the Uncle*), which was published in 1930, was the first Haitian novel to explore the life of the country's poor black farmers.

Haitian music is defined by the sound of the drum. Drums are used in both religious and secular performances. The standard drum used in vodou ceremonies is the rada (rah-DAH). Always found together in a set of three, the rada is made up of the mama (mah-MAH), the largest drum, which is struck with a wooden hammer; the seconde (seh-GOHND), which is struck with a baguette (bah-GET, a bow-shaped piece of wood strung with a cord); and the boula (boo-LAH) or kata (kah-TAH), the smallest of the three drums, which is hit with two sticks.

Rada drums are usually painted in the colors of the spirits to which they are dedicated and are easily recognizable by the wooden pegs or knobs inserted below the rim of the head to tighten the skin. Rada drums are considered to be sacred objects by vodou practitioners and when a set of drums is fashioned, a vodou rite has to be performed to consecrate the drums before they are used.

Drums that are played during carnival come in three types: a conical one about 3 feet high (0.9 m) tightened by crisscrossing ropes; a small cylindrical hand drum hung from a cord around the neck of the player; and a double-headed drum, beaten with sticks or bare hands.

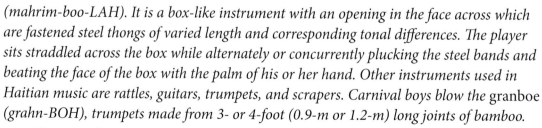

A distinctive Haitian instrument is the marimboula (mahrim-boo-LAH). It is a box-like instrument with an opening in the face across which are fastened steel thongs of varied length and corresponding tonal differences. The player sits straddled across the box while alternately or concurrently plucking the steel bands and beating the face of the box with the palm of his or her hand. Other instruments used in Haitian music are rattles, guitars, trumpets, and scrapers. Carnival boys blow the granboe (grahn-BOH), trumpets made from 3- or 4-foot (0.9-m or 1.2-m) long joints of bamboo.

The Spanish tambourine is as popular in Haiti as in the other Caribbean islands. The thumb of the right hand is covered with powdered resin and then drawn in a rapid spiral circling the face of the tambourine. The result is a humming roar that can be heard from far away.

Leon Laleau, a versatile writer who used both prose and poetry, portrayed the deep despair of his people in a literary piece, *Le Choc (The Shock)*. His *Musique Nègre (Negro Music)* is an excellent collection of verse expressing the heart and soul of the Haitian masses. The most famous Haitian writer, however, was Jacques Roumain, poet, novelist, and ethnologist. His novel, *Gouverneurs de la Rosée (Masters of the Dew)*, is a powerful and realistic portrayal of life in a poor rural community.

Women have always been active in Haiti's literary scene. Virginie Sampeur, Ida Faubert, and Lucie Archin-Lay were noted poets and essayists. The novelist Marie Chauvet, who died in 1973, was a major voice in Haitian literature. Today, one of the most prominent Haitian writers is Haitian-born Edwidge Danticat (b. 1969), author of *Krik? Krak!*

PAINTING

There are more than eight hundred recognized painters in Haiti, most of them self-taught, working full-time, and painting in a variety of styles. A unique style of painting is the Primitive movement, a naive style making use of bright colors and depicting the daily life of the Haitian population. This movement started in 1944, when DeWitt Peters, an artist and teacher from the United States, encouraged the renaissance of Haitian art by opening the Centre d'Art in Port-au-Prince. Within a few years, Haitian Primitive paintings received international recognition, and several outstanding Haitian paintings now form part of the permanent collection of New York City's Museum of Modern Art.

Philomé Obin, founder of the School of Cap-Haïtien and considered the founding father of the Primitive movement, was the first renowned Primitive painter; his masterpiece is entitled *The Funeral of Charlemagne Peralte*. But the greatest Primitive painter was probably Hector Hyppolite, a poor vodou priest who painted doors, windows, and buildings to earn a living. Every now and then, he used left-over house paint and brushes made from chicken feathers to paint pictures. His work was discovered in 1945 by DeWitt Peters. Hyppolite was brought to Port-au-Prince where he remained a prolific painter until his death in 1948.

"I come from a place where breath, eyes and memory are one, a place from which you carry your past like the hair on your head. Where women return to their children as butterflies or as tears in the eyes of the statues that their daughters pray to."
—Edwidge Danticat, from her novel *Breath, Eyes, Memory*

One of the most famous and well-respected contemporary Haitian writers is Edwidge Danticat, who is the author of over a dozen books. She was born in 1969 in Port-au-Prince, where she lived until age nine, at which point she moved to Brooklyn, New York. Her earliest writings reflected her disorientation brought on by the move from Haiti. Some of the prevailing themes in her work include what it means to be of Haitian descent, the relationships between mothers and daughters, and how one navigates the world with a bicultural identity. She has won many awards for her literature and has worked on projects about Haitian art as well as documentaries about Haiti. She remains a staunch advocate for issues affecting Haitians.

Her novels include Breath, Eyes, Memory *(1994),* The Dew Breaker *(2004), and* Claire of the Sea Light *(2013).* Krik? Krak! *(1996) is a collection of short stories, and* Brother, I'm Dying *(2007) is a memoir. In addition she has written several young adult novels and a picture book.*

Mural painting is also popular. The movement was started in 1949 by Selden Rodman, an American poet and art critic. Huge murals can be found on everything from church cathedrals and hotel walls to airports and exhibition sites.

The Episcopal Church gave a boost to Haitian painting when it commissioned the Centre d'Art to decorate its churches. The most acclaimed mural is Wilson Bigaud's *Miracle at Cana*, in which the New Testament feast is placed in a Haitian setting and embellished with such details as a policeman chasing a thief. This mural adorned the Episcopal Cathedral of the Holy Trinity in Port-au-Prince, until it was destroyed in the 2010 earthquake.

A boy walks by a mural of President Michel Martelly in Port-au-Prince in 2011.

ARCHITECTURE

Haitian architecture is a contrast of African heritage and French colonial style. When it comes to color, however, the style is pure Caribbean. Haitians reveal their imagination, love of fun, and lack of inhibitions as they cover all available surfaces with the sun-drenched hues of their tropical surroundings. Walls, doors, shutters, roofs, trim—even lamp posts and garbage cans—are painted with diamonds, squares, stripes, and solid panels in vividly contrasting colors.

Climate plays an important role in Haitian architecture. As in many Caribbean islands, houses in Haiti are sited in such a way that they can benefit as much as possible from the cooling trade winds blowing from east to west.

Certain architectural elements also help cope with the extremely hot weather—peaked roofs increase the protection from sun and rain, cut out trim filters out the bright sun while still allowing air to pass through,

and unglazed attic windows provide ventilated storage space for the family's harvest.

As in other French- and Spanish-influenced islands, balconies and front porches directly overlooking the street are common features, enabling Haitians to socialize easily with their neighbors. On narrow city streets, houses usually include a store or warehouse on the street level, while the family residence is located on the floor above.

In the countryside, people live in *cailles* (KAEE), which are simple, often one-room houses with roofs made of hay or corrugated iron.

All dwellings, whether rural or urban, are decorated with brightly painted doors, shutters, and woodwork.

In the wealthy suburban residential neighborhoods of the cities of Jacmel and Port-au-Prince, houses are set in large gardens and characterized by elegant gingerbread fretwork, delicate and ornate wooden or iron balconies, extravagant bell towers, and windows outlined in brick archways. Entire interior walls are sometimes covered with elaborately carved redwood panels.

Who would have ever dreamed that Haiti's most popular, most provocative, outlandish, diaper-wearing, cross-dressing pop star would run for president? He did, and he won. In 2010, the musician who went by the name Sweet Micky became Michel Martelly, the president of Haiti.

In 2015, near the end of Martelly's term, the documentary movie Sweet Micky for President *was released. Narrated by Pras Michel of the American hip-hop group The Fugees, the movie follows the unlikely candidate through the election. Presented with verve, attitude, enthusiasm, and great music, the movie has high entertainment value.*

Most critics find, however, that the film is one-sided. Pras Michel is a good friend of Martelly's, after all, and the question of whether Martelly had any credentials, other than popularity, to become president of a desperate country is not addressed. Nonetheless, the movie won both the audience award and jury award for documentary feature at the Slamdance Film Festival in 2015.

THE EIGHTH WONDER OF THE WORLD

Built as the crowning glory of King Henri Christophe's reign, the Citadelle Laferrière is the largest fortress ever built in the Western Hemisphere. Standing at the peak of a 3,000-foot (914 m) mountain, the Citadelle can only be reached by riding a mule.

Eccentric King Christophe, who ruled the north of Haiti from 1807 to 1820, was a great builder of castles and palaces. He built the Sans Souci Palace at the base of the mountain as a private retreat, but he embarked on the Citadelle with a loftier purpose in mind—it was intended to be a fortress against a French invasion of his kingdom.

Sitting on top of a mountain and shaped in an irregular square, the Citadelle Laferrière tapers to a prow. The walls, 80 to 130 feet (24 to 40 m) high and 20 to 30 feet (6 to 9 m) thick, surround a central parade ground, and 360 huge cannons guard all approaches. The fortress was designed to contain a garrison of 10,000 soldiers.

Work on the Citadelle started in 1804 and continued sporadically for the next fifteen years. It is alleged that 200,000 people were put to work on the fortress and over 20,000 of them died from exhaustion during construction.

But King Christophe's dream of seeing the building completed never came true. In 1821, the people revolted against him and he committed suicide. His wife and a loyal courtier carried his body to the Citadelle and dropped it in a vat of quicklime in the courtyard to fulfill his wish of being buried in his fortress.

Cannons surround the Citadelle fortress.

The Citadelle Laferrière was never completed and has never been used. Still, it is Haiti's most revered national symbol and is a monument to the lives sacrificed in the struggle for freedom.

Designated by the United Nations as one of the world's cultural treasures, the building is considered by some to be the eighth wonder of the world. However, neglect and the effect of the tropical climate have taken their toll and the stone-and-mortar structure is in dire need of repair.

Cap-Haïtien, Haiti's former capital, still has fountains, forts, and fine stone bridges built in the colonial style. One of the most beautiful examples is the neoclassic parish church, which was built in the eighteenth century.

SCULPTURE

Haitian sculpture blends African artistic heritage with the spontaneity and creativity of an uprooted people. Odilon Duperier, a former carpenter's assistant, excels in carved masks and figures. Jasmin Joseph is best known for his lively and imaginative terra-cotta sculptures and the choir screen he created for the Holy Trinity Cathedral. Georges Liautaud and Murat Brière, the foremost Primitive sculptors, specialize in sheet iron sculpture. Using scrap iron from old gas cans, they produce amazing sculptures blending reality and fantasy. One sculptor who makes use of a rather unusual medium is Roger François. This highly talented artist carves strikingly human faces out of dried roots.

INTERNET LINKS

www.biography.com/people/edwidge-danticat
Find a short bio on Haiti's foremost writer here.

news.bbc.co.uk/2/hi/in_pictures/8511340.stm
The BBC offers a slide show of Haitian artwork after the earthquake, including pictures of the Holy Trinity murals.

www.nytimes.com/2010/05/11/arts/design/11restore.html?pagewanted=1&ref=arts
This article is about rescuing the famous murals following the destruction of the Holy Trinity Episcopal Cathedral in Port-au-Prince.

www.sweetmickyforpresident.com
The official trailer for the movie can be seen here.

LEISURE

Men gather to play dominoes in a cockfighting arena in Dezemitte, an area of Pétionville in Port-au-Prince.

11

FOR THE ELITE IN PORT-AU-PRINCE, their social activities are similar to any other wealthy group's: dancing, banquets, golf, tennis, and swimming. For most Haitians, however, much simpler and less expensive pleasures are enjoyed. The house of the vodou priest serves as a kind of community center. The most common leisure activities for the poor are the vodou ceremony, which involves singing and dancing, as well as cockfighting, the national sport.

With Haiti's widespread illiteracy, a strong oral culture has arisen, so storytelling is another popular form of entertainment. Every region in Haiti has its *maître conte* (met COHNT), literally a "master of stories," who wanders from village to village, recounting stories and folktales passed down from one generation to the next.

What do children in Haiti do for fun? Can kids who are hungry and desperately poor even have fun? What do kids who live in tiny tin shacks, without electricity, never mind electronics, with no toys or sports equipment— what do those children do for fun? The answer is, they work, but they also play. They make up games, play and laugh, and act ... like kids.

SPORTS

The most popular sport played in Haiti is soccer, although the game has never aroused the same type of passionate following in Haiti as it has in some Latin American and other Caribbean countries.

In the countryside, children who cannot afford to buy a proper soccer ball are content to kick a substitute made of rags around an empty patch of ground. Competitive soccer is generally restricted to Port-au-Prince, where regular matches take place at the national Sylvio Cator stadium. The stadium was partly destroyed in the earthquake but has been renovated.

In spite of the lack of sporting facilities, the Haiti national soccer team qualified for the World Cup Tournament in 1974, but did not make it past the first round. More recently, the national team made it to the quarterfinals of the CONCACAF Gold Cup in 2015.

In general, conventional sports play only a limited part in recreational life, as they all require some form of equipment or location the average Haitian cannot afford. Tennis, for example, is only played by the urban upper and middle classes.

GAMBLING

The popularity of gambling and games of chance is the result of the Haitian's belief that so much depends on the fancy of the gods. Winners of bets are seen as the lucky ones chosen by the gods. Thus gambling is not only an attempt to make some money, but also an attempt to know the wishes of the gods.

Gambling is a predominantly male activity. Even those with little to spare will take their chances now and then. Large sums of money are won and lost in the casinos in Port-au-Prince, open only to the well-to-do. The rest of the population makes wagers on cockfights, bullfights, card games, or dominoes.

The most popular form of gambling is the lottery. Imported from the Spanish Antilles, the *loterie-borlette* (lot-tree bohr-LET) has superceded all other forms of gambling in Haiti. Tickets for the weekly draw are sold in all major town centers.

Dreams and minor incidents of daily life are interpreted in terms of winning numbers. A car accident might attract a huge crowd that buys lottery tickets based on a combination of the numbers on the license plates. During vodou ceremonies, Haitians implore the spirits to reveal winning lottery numbers.

BAMBOCHE

The *bamboche* (bahm-BOSH) is a social get-together with no sacred significance. In the countryside, bamboche takes place under a *tonnelle* (toh-NELL), a simple structure of poles supporting a banana-thatched roof. The whole village gathers to have a good time. The dancing is free, except for special occasions when money is collected for a feast. Money is also collected to buy rum. Participants usually buy refreshments and snacks from street vendors.

The bamboche is a social occasion for people to meet, and group dances are preferred. The dance is led by a dance master, usually the best dancer in the neighborhood. As older people are typically more skilled, they tend to be the leaders and the younger ones follow. The usual dances are congo pastoral, merengue, rumba, and bolero. In the towns, bamboches are sometimes held at open-air dance halls.

The closest thing to a national sport in Haiti is cockfighting. From March to December, cockfights take place every Sunday morning all over the country. The gaguère *(gah-GAIR), or fighting pit, is a kind of arena with terraced wooden benches all around.*

Only roosters are used in cockfights, and only men are the animal trainers. Fed all year with raw meat and hot peppers soaked in rum, the animals are aggressive and tough. The rooster's skin is rubbed with ginger to harden it, and the neck, feet, and rump are massaged with mahogany bark. The sharp spurs the

animals wear on their claws can inflict fatal wounds on the opposing rooster. To increase the chances of winning, they are given war-like names by their owners, such as Tambou Mèt *("Drums of the Master"),* Focsé Malhè *("There's Going to be a Disaster"), or* Consul Pangnol *("Spanish Consul").*

A cockfight usually ends with the death of the losing bird. Attended by people of all classes, the bouts evoke from spectators the frenzied enthusiasm that is lavished on soccer in many Latin American countries.

In the United States, cockfighting is illegal, because it is considered cruelty to animals. Nevertheless, the activity goes on secretly wherever there are large populations of Haitians or Latin communities who also revel in the sport.

COMBITE

Since black Haitian farmers often cannot afford to pay people to work for them, they get together in a *combite* (cohm-BIT) to help each other. On the appointed day, friends, relatives, and neighbors turn up at a person's house or field and help build a house or bring in the harvest. The helpers are not paid, but are offered rum and food after the job is done. Everyone sings as they work under the direction of an appointed leader. When a great number of workers are involved, they divide themselves into two teams and compete to see which team finishes first. Work ends in mid-afternoon, and the feast may conclude with a dance.

In another form of combite, a group of workers goes from place to place to help farmers. The combite then becomes a roving dance, stopping at the houses or farms of neighbors to assist in planting, reaping, or housebuilding. To the rhythm of singing and drum beating, the combite engages in the *chario-pie* (shah-rio-PIEH) movement, a constant halt and run. At the end of the day, everyone gathers under the tonnelle for a bamboche.

The combite is an essential part of rural life. It has an economic and social function, helping to knit the rural community into a self-reliant society.

INTERNET LINKS

www.abc.net.au/news/2010-02-07/cockfighting-survives-haitis-devastation/2572802
Even the earthquake couldn't stop the cockfight.

www.npr.org/templates/story/story.php?storyId=127114784
"In Battered Haiti, Cockfighting a Fierce Diversion" is available in text or audio.

www.vice.com/read/hatians-are-hooked-on-the-new-york-lotto-961
This is an eye-opening look at gambling in Haiti, with photos.

FESTIVALS

A woman in a glitzy costume dances in a Mardi Gras parade.

12

HAITIANS LOVE TO CELEBRATE. Religious and civic holidays are reasons for music and dance. Festivals are colorful events enjoyed by Haitians of all ages.

Some of the festivals celebrated in Haiti include Christmas, Mardi Gras, Spring Festival, and the Day of the Dead. Every event provides an opportunity for the Haitian people to bring out their musical instruments to accompany their songs and dances. A drum or a guitar, a bottle of rum, and perhaps a lively homemade costume are all that are required for a celebration and are within almost everyone's means.

Costumes for Carnival, or Kanaval, are festive and whimsical.

A child enjoys a gift of food and candy for Christmas.

CHRISTMAS

Christmas is a big event in Haiti. Everyone goes to Midnight Mass on Christmas Eve and then goes home for a celebration dinner and Christmas gifts. Naturally, every effort is made to prepare a special dinner on this day.

As in most of the Christian world, Haitian children believe that if they have been good, Santa Claus, or *Bonhomme Noël*, will visit and bring them presents. If they have been bad, however, *Père Fouettard*, Bonhomme Noël's companion in these visits, will leave a whip that their parents will use to beat them.

CHRISTMAS SIGHTS

Months before Christmas, children begin working on their fanal *(fah-NAHL) or Christmas lantern. Cardboard strips are glued together in the shape of a house or church. A design is drawn in pencil on the cardboard walls and then carefully punched out with a nail. Colored paper is pasted on the inside of the walls and when a lighted candle or small kerosene lamp is placed inside the fanal, the pattern stands out like stained glass. On Christmas Eve, boys and girls carry their fanals in a procession around the streets of the town or village. It's a wonderful sight, and many people come out to their doorsteps to watch the procession. When they get home, the children place the fanal near their windows so that passersby can catch its glow.*

Children also make nativity scenes at school. Cardboard figures of Joseph, Mary, Jesus, and the Wise Men are placed in a crèche. In some country towns, large nativity scenes are built in the town square and may feature public figures, such as the mayor or the tax collector!

Christmas trees are not common; they are popular only among the rich urban upper class. The custom was left behind by the Americans, who occupied Haiti before World War II. A more common sight is the decorated tonnelle in rural areas. Haitians hang gourds and strips of colored paper on the tonnelle to give it a festive atmosphere.

NEW YEAR'S DAY AND INDEPENDENCE DAY

New Year's Day is especially significant to Haitians. Not only does it signify the beginning of a new year, but it is also commemorates the beginning of freedom in the country as January 1 is also Haiti's Independence Day. In recognition of the importance of the occasion, January 2 is also a public holiday in the country.

On New Year's Day, entire Haitian families often gather for a special dinner of *soup joumou*, an aromatic pumpkin soup. Housewives put out the best tablecloth and dinnerware. Everyone in the family puts on a brand-new set of clothes, and children also receive gifts from their godparents.

The formal and solemn part of the holiday takes place in the morning, when wreaths and flowers are placed in front of the National Palace and at the foot of the Statue of the Maroon (a statue of a freed slave), a symbol of freedom for Haiti's black people. In Port-au-Prince, marches are organized in celebration of the country's independence from colonial rule.

People celebrate New Year's Day and Haitian Independence Day in Port-au-Prince.

THE RARA

Rara bands appear during Lent, the period between Carnival—which ends with Mardi Gras—and Easter. Wearing colored shirts and carrying a red flag, they dance their way down the streets in the mountains and villages. Sometimes they carry a dead chicken on a stick or lanterns made of tins filled with kerosene.

Rara bands dance and sing to the beat of drums. For small gifts of money, they will dance for onlookers. The leaders are accomplished dancers dressed like jesters with brightly colored handkerchiefs and sequined capes. When two groups meet, their leaders sometimes challenge each other to competitive dances.

Near the town of Jérémie, Rara festivities include exhibitions by wrestlers, who are sometimes accompanied by their own musicians. During Holy Week, the Rara carry an effigy of Judas Iscariot from place to place. On Good Friday, the effigy is hidden, and the community makes merry as it hurries about in search of the hiding place so the villainous effigy can be destroyed. The Rara do not dance on Easter Sunday.

On January 2, a tall pole is erected in the center of town, and money and cakes are placed on top of the pole. Many young men try to climb the pole to get to the money and cakes, but the pole is greased, and only the best athletes succeed in reaching the top.

January 1	Independence Day
January 2	Ancestors' Day
Variable	Kanaval/Carnival
Variable	Shrove Tuesday
Variable	Good Friday
April 7	Anniversary of the Death of Toussaint
April 14	Pan-American Day
May 1	Agriculture and Labor Day
May 18	Flag and University Day
Variable	Corpus Christi
July 16	Saut d'Eau Pilgrimage
July 25	St. James' Day/Ogou Day
July 26	Festival of St. Anne/Erzulie
October 17	Anniversary of the Death of Dessalines
October 24	United Nations Day
November 1	All Saints' Day
November 2	Fete Gede/Day of the Dead/All Souls' Day
November 18	Battle of Vetieres' Day
December 25	Christmas Day

KANAVAL

Kanaval, or Carnival, begins every year on January 6 and culminates in a four-day party that ends on Mardi Gras (Shrove Tuesday) with a parade. In Creole, the parade is called *Defile Kanaval*. The largest one is held annually in Port-au-Prince, with smaller *defiles* held in other locations around the country.

Preparations begin as early as October, with adults and children making their own masks. Every Sunday between January 6 and Lent, there are

On July 16, the little town of Ville Bonheur ("Happiness Town") swarms with fifty thousand-strong crowds that have come from all over Haiti to celebrate the Saut d'Eau (soh DOH, "waterfall") festival. The Virgin Mary is reported to have appeared at the top of a palm tree near the waterfall in the nineteenth century. Today tens of thousands of pilgrims come to pray to the Virgin and at the same time tell their sorrows to the vodou spirits. In long lines, they make their way to the rock where La Tombe River falls in a cascade. Standing under the gushing water, they hope to wash away their bad luck. One after another, silently, they come down from the waterfall with tears streaming down their cheeks.

Nearby, the presence of gaming tables and the sound of beating drums give an air of carnival to the gathering. But this notion is quickly dispelled by the chorus of supplications coming from the parish church.

processions in the streets with singing, carnival bands playing drums, and trumpets. The bands dance their way down the street, and people from all around join them, dancing and singing. Starting on the Sunday before Lent, the carnival starts to get more and more elaborate. There are parades with flamboyantly decorated floats, and wealthy families organize grand fancy dress balls. Some towns elect a king and queen of the Carnival.

During Kanaval, young boys run around in masks and costumes. Blowing whistles, they stop passersby and offer them a look inside their *lamayoe* (lah-mah-YOT) in return for a few cents. A lamayote is a box containing a pet animal or 'monster,' usually a lizard, a mouse, or a bug.

Traditionally, Haitians burn their costumes on the last day of Carnival. In reality, all but the wealthy now save their costumes for the following year.

SPRING FESTIVAL

The Spring Festival runs from May 1 to 4. Less elaborate than the Mardi Gras Carnival, it is usually celebrated with feasting and dancing. Each town organizes a parade, and even the mayor joins in the march.

BARON SAMEDI

Baron Samedi or "Baron Saturday" is the male loa of death and the custodian of cemeteries in vodou. He and his wife, the loa Maman Brigitte, are regarded as the spiritual parents of the departed. In rituals held on the Day of the Dead, vodou worshippers pray, give offerings, and invoke Baron Samedi, in order to communicate with the dead. Similar to the way that the loa Legba connects loas to the living, Baron Samedi acts as a bridge between the world of the dead and the world of the living.

Baron Samedi is often depicted as a tall man dressed in a funereal black coat and top hat. Believers have great respect for the Baron, since he is the loa of death. Supposedly, the late President François Duvalier dressed himself to look like Baron Samedi to intimidate the citizenry.

There is, however, another side to Baron Samedi. According to vodou beliefs, Baron Samedi dislikes ending the lives of children. As a protector of children, vodou priests and priestesses will call upon him to heal sick children.

Labor Day, or Agriculture Day, is part of the Spring Festival celebrations. It was first decreed a holiday in the nineteenth century by President Alexandre Pétion, who hoped to stimulate an interest in agriculture. In those days, the best laborer in each parish received a prize, while a child from the best-cultivated farm in the district was awarded free education by the state. Today there are no competitions, but the day is still observed as a holiday.

FETE GEDE

Wakes and funerals are occasions of social importance, where the departed is entertained by feasting and drinking, storytelling, and the playing of cards and other games. But on November 2, the entire day is given over to celebrating and honoring the dead.

All Souls' Day, or Fete Gede (Day of the Dead), is one of the four biggest holidays in Haiti. People everywhere visit cemeteries with tributes of flowers and say prayers for their dead ancestors. Gifts may include homemade beeswax candles and bottles stuffed with chili peppers, which are meant to warm the bones of the dead.

At home, it is customary to *manger aux morts* (mahn-djay oh MORH), or offer food to the family's dead ancestors. Some people place the food on the ground, while others put it on the table where the dead person used to sit. A candle is lit and prayers are said. Only after the food has been offered to the dead does the rest of the family sit down to dinner.

HARVEST DAYS

Harvest festivals best exemplify the influence of vodou on daily life in Haiti. For two days in November, Haitian farmers celebrate *manger-yam* (mahn-djay YAM), literally "eat yam day," a vodou ritual that points to the importance of yams in the diet of the rural population.

One of the recreational high points of the year, manger-yam is celebrated with feasting, drinking, singing, and dancing. A vodou priest performs a ceremony marked by incantations to the dead and to the vodou spirits.

People offer food and drink to the spirits on November 1 during a vodou ceremony celebrating Fete Gede.

INTERNET LINKS

www.godchecker.com/pantheon/caribbean-mythology.php?deity=BARON-SAMEDI

This is a quick portrait of Baron Samedi.

www.timeanddate.com/holidays/haiti

The year's calendar of holidays is found here.

FOOD

In the slum of Cité Soleil, a young girl carries bananas on her head through streets flooded by Tropical Storm Noel.

13

THE CHASM BETWEEN RICH AND poor, as with so many aspects of Haitian life, is evident in the quantity and quality of the food consumed by the opposite social classes. The urban elite can gorge on rich Creole cuisine, while the poor often eat only one paltry meal per day.

At its best, Haitian food is cooked with fresh ingredients and local herbs and spices, with many special dishes that are the equal of the best cuisines in the world. The African, French, and Spanish influences give Haitian cuisine an elegance and range that many believe is unmatched in the region.

A woman bakes clay "biscuits" under the sun in Cité Soleil.

When times are particularly rough, which seems to be all the time, Haiti's poorest people often resort to literally eating dirt to relieve their hunger pangs. Merchants truck a clay-like dirt into town; women buy the dirt and then process it into mud cookies to sell. The cookies, or biscuits, are made of vegetable shortening, salt, and mud, and dried in the sun.

THE CREOLE PIG

The Creole pig was a species of pig indigenous to Haiti, now extinct. As livestock, they were well-adapted to the climate and conditions present in rural Haiti. They were used as food, slaughtered as payment for marriages, emergencies, school, or vodou ceremonies. In 1983, African swine fever hit the pig population of the neighboring Dominican Republic, there was serious concern that the flu could spread to Haiti and the United States. Along with USAID (US Agency for International Development) the Haitian authorities slaughtered all the Creole pigs. Less hardy white pigs were imported from the United States as replacements, but Haitians were either unable to afford the new pigs or saw many of them die from disease. Many farmers consequently suffered a drop in their standard of living. Recently there have been attempts to breed a pig with similar characteristics and qualities of the Creole pig. If these efforts succeed, it would be a victory for a group of people that has little to celebrate.

A woman carries mangoes for sale.

THE HAITIAN DIET

The Haitian diet is high in starch. The staple foods are rice (grown locally in the Artibonite Valley since 1941), corn, millet, and yam. The Haitian national dish and the mainstay of Haitian cooking is *riz et pois* (rees eht PWAH), rice and beans. Most poor people eat *petit mil* (peh-tih MILL), or sorghum, which is pounded with a 20-pound (9-kg) pestle and cooked in an old, well-seasoned black iron bowl; every bit is scraped out for the family meal.

Green vegetables and tropical fruits grow well in Haiti, and a wide variety is available seasonally. However, vegetables do not make their way to the farmer's dinner table very often as farmers usually need to sell their produce for money or trade it for goods rather than eat it themselves. For vegetables, farmers eat the wild greens that they gather in open fields. Citrus fruits, avocados, breadfruit, and mangoes grow in abundance and are eaten extensively when in season. Mangoes are of particular importance in the Haitian diet as they are rich in vitamin A.

Meat is almost nonexistent in the diet of ordinary Haitians because of its high cost. Farmers often rear their own chickens, but again they tend to sell the eggs and meat rather than eat them. The most common meats consumed are goat and chicken. Fish and shellfish abound in the seas surrounding Haiti and in the rivers, but they are not usually eaten outside Port-au-Prince.

HAITIAN MEALTIME

Haitian farmers start the day at dawn with a breakfast of strong locally grown coffee, sometimes accompanied by a slice of sour bread baked from bitter manioc flour. (Bread made from imported wheat flour is almost non-existent outside urban centers.) A light lunch is eaten in the fields at midday. The principal meal of the day is eaten at home in the late afternoon with the whole family. It is usually the national dish of rice and beans, or a stew with a small piece of meat if the family's financial circumstances are favorable.

However, in the summer season, when the crops have not yet reached maturity, many rural people subsist on no more than one starchy meal a day, such as porridge made from corn, rice, or sorghum. To satisfy their hunger pangs, some people chew on sugarcane stalks or green mangoes.

A vendor selling live chickens carries them on his back.

CREOLE CUISINE

Much like the food of New Orleans, Haitian Creole cooking features distinctive recipes and subtle flavors imparted by the use of local herbs and spices.

Among the Creole specialties prepared in hotels, expensive restaurants, and upper-class homes are spiced shrimp, pheasant with orange sauce, green-turtle steak, wild duck, and salad made with hearts of palm.

Rice *djon-djon* (jon-JON), one of Haiti's rice-and-bean dishes, is found

Rice and beans is a Haitian staple, as it is throughout Latin America.

nowhere else in the Caribbean as it calls for an ingredient that is unique to Haiti—Haitian black mushrooms. The inedible stems of these small mushrooms are used to color the rice black and then removed, leaving the mushroom caps, which are added along with lima beans.

Another traditional Haitian dish is *calalou* (kah-lah-LOO), a mixture of salted pork, crabmeat, peppers, onions, spinach, okra, and chili pepper. The ingredients are simmered for one hour or more, and the dish is served with rice.

Other dishes are *tassot* (tah-SOH), a preparation of grilled meat, and *pain patate* (pahn pah-TAT), a pudding made of grated potato, figs, bananas, and sugar.

Numerous sauces are used to spice up Haitian meals. The most renowned of these is *timalice* (tih-mah-LISS), an extremely spicy tomato and onion concoction.

Typical beverages include a mild variety of coffee that is grown locally and is mainly consumed by upper- and middle-class Haitians, soft drinks made of brightly colored syrups and shaved ice, and alcoholic drinks, such as whiskey, brandy, and the locally distilled Barbencourt rum.

SUGAR

Sugar, consumed in enormous quantities, helps to make up for the lack of caloric content in the typical Haitian diet, but not for its lack of protein and vitamins.

Rapadou (rah-pah-DOO) is a syrup produced in the refining process of sugar. It is used to sweeten drinks, tea, and coffee. Rapadou is also the base for *clairin*, the raw and concentrated rum that is the most popular alcoholic beverage among rural Haitians.

A large amount of sugar is also consumed by chewing stalks of sugarcane. Both adults and children pluck the stalks directly from the field or buy them

Haiti's cuisine represents the best of its varied and multiple influences. While similar to the rest of the Latin-Caribbean, Haitian food is unique in its boldness and spice, representing its African foundation. But the colonial French influence is apparent in its sophistication of technique.

The effect of Caribbean geography is apparent in the use of fish, shellfish and native fruits and vegetables, such as coconuts, plantains, mangoes, limes, okra, beans, yams, and cassava. Beans or other legumes used in the daily fare of rice and beans are native to the Western Hemisphere and were staples for indigenous peoples.

The legacy of poverty is obvious by the use of dried and smoked fish in many dishes. Unless they live by the sea, Haitians do not eat fresh fish as it requires refrigeration. Goat and chicken are the most commonly used meats when meat is featured in a meal, because these animals require little supervision and can forage for themselves.

at the market, tear off the leaves, and chew on the stalks with the bark still on to extract the sweet juice, which is refreshing in the hot Haitian climate.

True to their French origins, upper- and middle-class Haitians love sweets and pastries, and always keep them in stock. No dinner is complete without a sweet dessert, such as a rich mousse or ice cream.

THE MARKETPLACE

Markets are the center of economic and social activity in many towns and villages. In the Port-au-Prince area, market vendors make their way to one of the twenty-three markets as early as 5:00 a.m. Many women walk several miles carrying huge baskets on their heads to sell the produce they have grown and buy the food and manufactured goods they need.

Sugar cane can be a sweet treat.

The newly rebuilt Iron Market is a shining model of hope in earthquake-ravaged Port-au-Prince.

The Iron Market, which is packed with thousands of Haitians every day, is the heart and soul of Port-au-Prince. In the countryside, markets are just wide open spaces where women gather to trade their wares. Farmer women display their vegetables and fruits on long tables and set in neat rows. Salted codfish and manioc flour are piled into towering mounds, and meat is sold in the open since there are no refrigerated containers.

In addition to food, a wide variety of other goods are offered for sale: fabrics, baskets, locally-made cigarettes, contraband whiskey, straw hats, cooking utensils, lamps made from old tin cans, spices, and rum. The marketplace is noisy and bustling with activity, with customers haggling over prices and sellers praising their wares.

Prepared foods, such as bread, fried bananas, and grilled meats, are also sold. The most popular market-stall dish is a porridge made with ground corn, sugar, and milk. It is cooked in a big tin can over a wood fire. Served in a tin cup and eaten on the spot with a teaspoon, this porridge is consumed at any time of the day.

Food vendors sell their wares inside the new Iron Market.

INTERNET LINKS

www.tatimiya.com/2014/03/salad.html
Tati Miya offers a history of Haitian cuisine, info about vodou, many authentic recipes, and much more.

www.whats4eats.com/caribbean/haiti-cuisine
Recipes for some common Haitian dishes are here.

HAITIAN POTATO SALAD

4 potatoes, peeled and cubed

1 carrot, peeled and chopped

1 small beet

2 hard-boiled eggs, peeled and coarsely chopped

½ cup (75 grams) sweet peas (frozen and thawed)

½ medium onion, minced

1/3 cup (50 g) red bell pepper, diced

1/3 cup (50 g) green bell pepper, diced

2 Tablespoons mayonnaise

1 Tbsp apple cider vinegar

salt and pepper to taste

Boil potatoes and carrot in water with 1 teaspoon salt for 10 minutes or until tender.

Boil beet separately in water with 1 teaspoon salt until tender, then peel and chop into small cubes.

In a bowl, place cubed potatoes, diced beet, chopped eggs, sweet peas, carrots, onion, red and green bell peppers, and mix gently with mayonnaise and vinegar. Add salt and black pepper.

SOUP JOUMOU (HAITIAN PUMPKIN SOUP)

This savory pumpkin soup is served in Haiti on January 1, the anniversary of Haiti's liberation from France. In this recipe, butternut or kabocha squash stands in for Caribbean pumpkin.

2 cloves garlic

2 scallions, sliced, plus more for garnish

¼ cup roughly chopped parsley

½ tsp. dried thyme

1 medium shallot, sliced

Juice of 1 lime, plus wedges for serving

Kosher salt and freshly ground black pepper, to taste

1 lb. (.5 kg) beef chuck, cut into 1-inch pieces

2 tbsp. olive oil

1 butternut or ½ small kabocha squash, peeled and cut into 1-inch pieces

8 cups (2 liters) beef stock

1 scotch bonnet chile, left whole

2 carrots, peeled and cut into bite-sized pieces

2 stalks celery, chopped

1 small leek, trimmed, halved lengthwise, and cut into 1-inch (2.5 cm) pieces;

1 small yellow onion, peeled and coarsely chopped

1 large Yukon gold potato, peeled and cut into bite-sized pieces

1 medium turnip, peeled and cut into bite-sized pieces

½ small green cabbage, cored, sliced, and chopped

¼ pound (115 g) thin spaghetti

Puree garlic, scallions, parsley, thyme, shallots, lime juice, salt and pepper, and ½ cup water in a blender until smooth; mix with beef in a bowl, cover with plastic wrap, and refrigerate at least 4 hours or overnight.

Cover squash with water and bring to a boil in a saucepan over high heat; reduce heat to medium-low and cook, covered, until squash is tender, about 10 minutes. Drain, reserving ½ cup cooking liquid and transfer squash and liquid to a blender; puree until smooth and set aside.

Remove beef from marinade and dry with paper towels; set aside. Heat oil in a large stockpot over medium-high heat. Add beef; cook, turning as needed, until browned, about 8 minutes. Add stock and bring to a boil; reduce heat to medium, and cook, stirring occasionally, until beef is tender, about 1 ½ hours. Add whole chili, carrots, celery, leeks, onion, potatoes, turnips, and cabbage; cook, slightly covered and stirring occasionally, until vegetables are tender, about 20 minutes. Remove chili and discard. Add spaghetti, broken into pieces, and cook until tender.

Stir in reserved squash puree; cook, stirring occasionally, until soup is slightly thick, 5 minutes more; season with salt and pepper and serve with scallions and lime wedges.

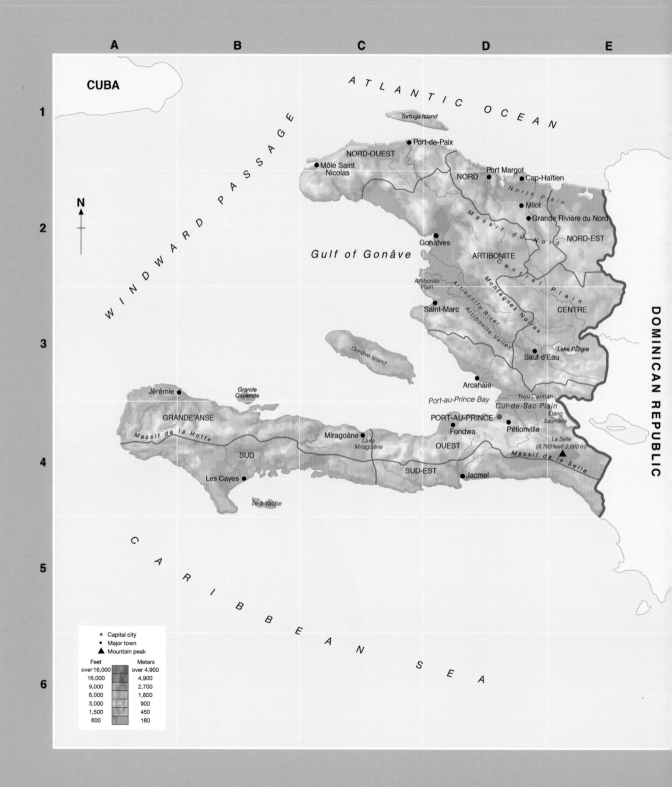

CUBA

ATLANTIC OCEAN

Tortuga Island

Port-de-Paix

NORD-OUEST

Môle Saint
Nicolas

NORD

Port Margot

Cap-Haïtien

North Plain

Milot

Massif du Nord

Grande Rivière du Nord

NORD-EST

Gonaïves

Gulf of Gonâve

ARTIBONITE

Central Plain

*Artibonite
Plain*

Saint-Marc

Artibonite River

Artibonite Valley

Montagnes Noires

Lake Péligre

CENTRE

Saut d'Eau

Gonâve Island

Arcahaie

Port-au-Prince Bay

Trou Caiman

Cul-de-Sac Plain

Jérémie

*Grande
Cayemite*

GRANDE'ANSE

PORT-AU-PRINCE

Fondwa

Pétionville

Étang
Saumâtre

Massif de la Hotte

Miragoâne

*Lake
Miragoâne*

SUD

OUEST

La Selle
(8,793 feet/ 2,680 m)

Massif de la Selle

Les Cayes

SUD-EST

Jacmel

Île-à-Vache

WINDWARD PASSAGE

N

DOMINICAN REPUBLIC

CARIBBEAN SEA

Capital city
Major town
Mountain peak

Feet		Meters
over 16,000		over 4,900
16,000		4,900
9,000		2,700
6,000		1,800
3,000		900
1,500		450
600		180

MAP OF HAITI

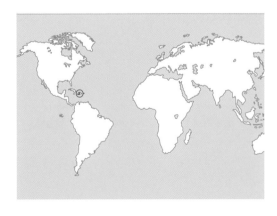

ECONOMIC HAITI

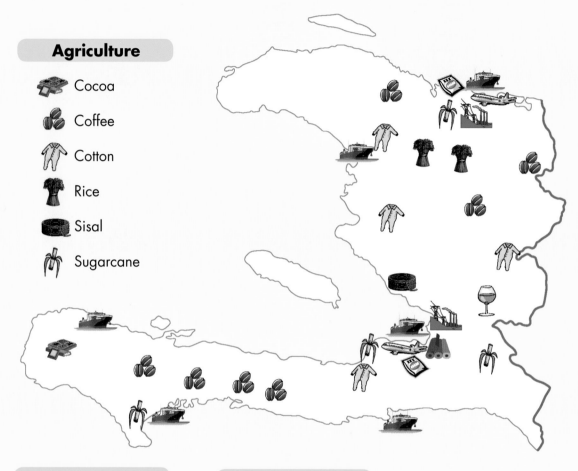

Agriculture

- Cocoa
- Coffee
- Cotton
- Rice
- Sisal
- Sugarcane

Manufacturing

- Rum
- Sugar Processing
- Textiles

Services

- Airport
- Port
- Power Plant

ABOUT THE ECONOMY

OVERVIEW

Poverty, corruption, vulnerability to natural disasters, and low levels of education for much of the population are among Haiti's most serious impediments to economic growth. Haiti's economy suffered a severe setback in January 2010 when a 7.0 magnitude earthquake destroyed much of its capital city, Port-au-Prince, and neighboring areas. Haiti suffers from a lack of investment, partly because of weak infrastructure such as access to electricity. Haiti's outstanding external debt was canceled by donor countries following the 2010 earthquake, but has since risen to $1.43 billion as of December 2014.

GROSS DOMESTIC PRODUCT (GDP)

$18.3 billion (2014)

GDP SECTORS

Services, 55 percent; agriculture, 25 percent; industry 20 percent (2014)

NATURAL RESOURCES

Bauxite, copper, calcium carbonate, gold, marble, hydropower

AGRICULTURAL PRODUCTS

Coffee, mangoes, sugarcane, rice, corn, cocoa, sorghum, wood, vetiver

CURRENCY

1 Haitian gourde (HTG) = 100 centimes
Notes: 500, 250, 100, 50, 25, 10, 5, 2, 1 gourde
Coins: 5, 1 gourdes; 50, 20, 10, 5 centimes
USD 1 = HTG 51.68 (September 2015)

INDUSTRIES

Sugar refining, flour milling, textiles, cement, light assembly of imported parts

WORKFORCE

4.8 million (2014)

MAJOR AIRPORTS

Hugo Chávez International Airport, Cap-Haïtien Airport

MAJOR PORTS

Cap-Haïtien, Gonaïves, Jacmel, Jérémie, Le Cayes, Miragoane, Port-au-Prince, Port-de-Paix, Saint-Marc

MAJOR EXPORTS

Apparel, oils, cocoa, mangoes, coffee

MAJOR IMPORTS

Food, manufactured goods, machinery and transport equipment, fuels, raw materials

MAJOR TRADE PARTNERS

United States, Dominican Republic, Canada

UNEMPLOYMENT RATE

41 percent (2010)

INFLATION RATE

3.9 percent (2014)

CULTURAL HAITI

Cap Haïtien
A former capital of Haiti, this city is famed for its eighteenth-century neoclassical church and artisan's market.

Plaine du Nord
The pilgrimage to celebrate St. James, or Ogou, on July 25, culminates in a ritual where devotees bathe themselves in a sacred mud pool.

The Citadelle Laferriere
The Citadelle and the Sans Souci Palace were both constructed by King Henri Christophe after Haitian independence. The Citadelle, although never completed, is a UNESCO World Heritage Site and considered by some to be a wonder of the world.

Limonade
This town is the site of a pilgrimage to celebrate the vodou spirit of love, Erzulie, on July 26.

Ville Bonheur
Vodou devotees bathe themselves in a waterfall during the festival of the Saut d'Eau pilgrimage on July 16, a day which marks a visitation by the Virgin Mary to this site.

Jacmel
Visitors to this town can admire Haiti's architectural heritage from the colonial architecture and Victorian gingerbread houses that are found in this town.

Port-au-Prince
Many of the former cultural buildings were destroyed in the earthquake, including the Episcopal Cathedral of the Holy Trinity, home of numerous important murals painted by some of the masters of Haitian art.

Pétionville
This upscale neighborhood near Port-au-Prince is known for its fine French restaurants and its galleries of Haitian art.

ABOUT THE CULTURE

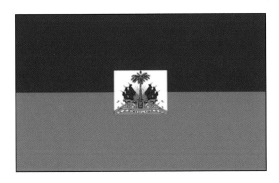

OFFICIAL NAME
Republic of Haiti

CAPITAL
Port-au-Prince

OTHER MAJOR CITIES
Cap Haïtien, Gonaïves, and Les Cayes

GOVERNMENT
Elected government

NATIONAL FLAG
Two equal horizontal bands of blue (top) and red with a centered white rectangle bearing the coat of arms, which contains a palm tree flanked by flags and two cannons above a scroll bearing the motto *L'union Fait La Force* ("Union Makes Strength")

NATIONAL ANTHEM
La Dessalinienne

POPULATION
10.1 million (2014)

OFFICIAL LANGUAGES
French and Creole

LITERACY RATE
61 percent (2014)

ETHNIC GROUPS
Black, 95 percent; mulatto and white, 5 percent

RELIGIOUS GROUPS
Roman Catholic 80 percent, vodou 50—70 percent*, other 3 percent, none 1 percent (*note: many Haitians both belong to the Catholic faith and practice vodou)

IMPORTANT ANNIVERSARIES
Independence Day (January 1), Anniversary of the Death of Dessalines (October 17), Battle of Vertieres Day (November 18)

LEADERS IN POLITICS
François Duvalier (president 1957—1971)
Jean-Claude Duvalier (president 1971—1986)
Jean-Bertrand Aristide (president 1990—1995, 2000—2004),
Boniface Alexandre (president 2004—2006)
René Préval (president 2006—2011)
Michel Martelly (president 2011—present)

TIMELINE

IN HAITI	IN THE WORLD
700 BCE–500 CE Migration of Ostionoid people from smaller Caribbean islands to Hispaniola	**753 BCE** Rome is founded.
500–1492 CE Development of Taino/Arawak settlements on Hispaniola	**116–117 CE** The Roman Empire reaches its greatest extent, under Emperor Trajan.
	600 CE Height of Mayan civilization
1492 Christopher Columbus lands at Cap Haïtien.	**1000** The Chinese perfect gunpowder and begin to use it in warfare.
1496 Spanish establish first European settlement in the Western Hemisphere at Santo Domingo.	**1530** Beginning of trans-Atlantic slave trade organized by the Portuguese in Africa.
	1620 Pilgrims sail the *Mayflower* to America.
1697 Spain cedes western part of Hispaniola to France as part of Treaty of Ryswick.	**1776** US Declaration of Independence
1791 The Boukman slave revolt erupts, leading to a full-scale rebellion led by Toussaint Louverture.	**1789–1799** The French Revolution
1801 Toussaint Louverture takes control of western Hispaniola and abolishes slavery.	
1804 Independence declared by General Dessalines; country is named Haiti.	
1818–1843 Jean-Pierre Boyer unifies Haiti.	
1862 The United States grants Haiti diplomatic recognition.	**1861** The US Civil War begins.
	1914 World War I begins.
1915–1934 The United States invades and occupies Haiti.	**1939** World War II begins.

IN HAITI	IN THE WORLD
	1945 World War II ends.
1956 Vodou physician François "Papa Doc" Duvalier seizes power in military coup.	**1957** The Russians launch *Sputnik*.
1964 Duvalier declares himself president-for-life.	**1966–69** The Chinese Cultural Revolution
1971 Duvalier dies, is succeeded by son Jean-Claude ("Baby Doc")	
1986 Baby Doc flees Haiti in the wake of mounting popular discontent.	**1986** Nuclear power disaster at Chernobyl in Ukraine
1990 Jean-Bertrand Aristide elected president.	
1991 Aristide ousted in a military coup.	**1991** Break-up of the Soviet Union
1994 Military regime resigns. Aristide returns.	
1995 Aristide disbands the armed forces.	**1997** Hong Kong is returned to China.
2000 Aristide elected president for a second term.	**2001** Terrorists crash planes in New York, Washington, DC, and Pennsylvania.
2004 Aristide is forced into exile by a rebel uprising. Hurricane Jeanne kills nearly 3,000.	**2003** War in Iraq
2008 Tropical storms and hurricanes kill 800.	**2008** Barack Obama elected president of the United States.
2010 Approximately 300,000 are killed by earthquake near Port-au-Prince.	
2011 Michel Martelly becomes president.	
2015 Mass deportation of Haitians from Dominican Republic.	**2015** Cuba and United States normalize diplomatic relations.

GLOSSARY

affranchis (ah-frahn-SHEE)
Freed former slaves who were granted French citizenship.

bamboche (bahm-BOSH)
Social get-together with dancing and drinking.

buccaneers
French and English pirates who attacked Spanish ships in the Caribbean during the seventeenth century.

coup d'état (koo day-TAHT)
A sudden, sometimes violent, overthrow of a government by a small group, usually with the help or backing of the military.

gro-bon-ange (groh-bohn-NAHNGE)
The soul, in vodou theology.

grosneg (groh NEGG)
A person of wealth and power.

houngan (hoon-GAHN)
Male vodou priest.

indigenous
Native to a place or location.

loas (LWAH)
In vodou, spirits with which human beings can communicate and which exert an influence on human life.

mambo (mahm-BOH)
Female priestess in vodou, proficient in faith healing.

mulattos
Mixed-race descendants of European colonists and African people who were brought to Haiti as slaves.

négritude (nay-grih-TUHD)
A commitment to pride in being black and in having a shared African heritage.

Rara
Bands that sing and dance during Lent.

taptaps (TAP-taps)
Trucks converted into buses with colorful decorations; most common form of transportation in rural areas.

tonnelle (toh-NELL)
A roofed structure used for village gatherings.

Tontons Macoutes (tohn-tohn mah-KOOT)
Private army set up by the Duvalier regime; known for its brutality.

vevers (veh-VAIR)
In vodou, patterns drawn on the ground using cornmeal to ward against evil spirits.

vodou
"The people's religion," combining ancestor worship, African animist beliefs, and Roman Catholic rituals.

zombie
A body without a soul that will do the bidding of its master.

FOR FURTHER INFORMATION

BOOKS

Danticat, Edwidge. *After the Dance: A Walk Through Carnival in Jacmel, Haiti* (Updated). New York: Vintage, reprint edition, 2015.

Dubois, Laurent. *Avengers of the New World: The Story of the Haitian Revolution*. Cambridge: The Belknap Press, 2005.

Dubois, Laurent. *Haiti: The Aftershocks of History*. New York: Picador, 2013.

Farmer, Paul. *The Uses of Haiti*. Monroe, Maine: Common Courage Press, 2003.

Katz, Jonathan M. *The Big Truck That Went By: How the World Came to Save Haiti and Left Behind a Disaster*. New York: St. Martin's Griffin, 2014.

Kidder, Tracy. *Mountains Beyond Mountains: The Quest of Dr. Paul Farmer, a Man Who Would Cure the World*. New York: Random House, 2009.

Wilentz, Amy. *Farewell, Fred Voodoo: A Letter from Haiti*. New York: Simon & Schuster, 2013.

DVDS/FILMS

Aristide and the Endless Revolution. Baraka Productions, 2012.

The Agronomist. New Line Home Video, 2005.

Egalite for All: Toussaint Louverture and the Haitian Revolution. PBS, 2009.

Frontline: Battle for Haiti. PBS, 2011

MUSIC

Boukman Eksperyans. *Kalfou Danjere*. Mercury Records, 2013

Michel Martelly "Sweet Micky." *Les Plus Grands Succès*. Hits Anthology Vols. 1 and 2. Essential Media Group, 2014.

Wyclef Jean. *Welcome to Haiti: Kreyole 101*. KOCH Records, 2004

WEBSITES

BBC News. Haiti Country Profile. news.bbc.co.uk/2/hi/americas/country_profiles/1202772.stm

BBC News, Haiti profile—Timeline. www.bbc.com/news/world-latin-america-19548814

Haitian Times, The. haitiantimes.com

CIA World Factbook. www.cia.gov/library/publications/the-world-factbook/geos/ha.html

New York Times, The. Times Topics, Haiti. topics.nytimes.com/top/news/international/countriesandterritories/haiti/index.html

Lonely Planet. Haiti. www.lonelyplanet.com/haiti

Embassy of the Republic of Haiti in Washington, DC   www.haiti.org

BIBLIOGRAPHY

BBC News, Haiti profile—Timeline. www.bbc.com/news/world-latin-america-19548814

BBC News. Haiti country profile. news.bbc.co.uk/2/hi/americas/country_profiles/1202772.stm

CDC. "Cholera in Haiti: One Year Later." www.cdc.gov/haiticholera/haiti_cholera.htm

CIA World Factbook. Haiti. www.cia.gov/library/publications/the-world-factbook/geos/ha.html

Immigration to the United States. "Haitian Boat People." immigrationtounitedstates.org/536-haitian-boat-people.html

Laurent, Olivier. "Haiti Earthquake: Five Years After." *Time*. January 12, 2015 time.com/3662225/haiti-earthquake-five-year-after

O'Malley, Martin. "U.N. should take responsibility for Haiti's deadly cholera epidemic." CNN, August 17, 2015. www.cnn.com/2015/08/17/opinions/omalley-haiti-cholera-un

Pallardy, Richard. "Haiti earthquake of 2010." *Encyclopaedia Britannica*. www.britannica.com/event/Haiti-earthquake-of-2010

Reuters. "Thousands of Haitians fleeing Dominican Republic stuck in camps." *The Guardian*, August 5, 2015. www.theguardian.com/world/2015/aug/05/thousands-of-haitians-fleeing-dominican-republic-stuck-in-camps

United States Department of State, OSAC. "Haiti 2014 Crime and Safety Report." www.osac.gov/pages/ContentReportDetails.aspx?cid=15745

Water.org. Haiti. water.org/country/haiti

INDEX

INDEX